SITTING BULL, PRISONER OF WAR

SOUTH DAKOTA

STATE HISTORICAL SOCIETY

PRESS   PIERRE

PRISONER OF WAR

SITTING BULL,

BY DENNIS C. POPE

This publication is funded, in part, by
the Great Plains Education Foundation, Inc., Aberdeen, S.Dak.

Library of Congress Cataloging-in-Publication data
Pope, Dennis C., 1934-
Sitting Bull, prisoner of war / by Dennis C. Pope.
    p. cm.
Includes bibliographical references and index.
ISBN 978-0-9822749-4-1
1. Sitting Bull, 1831-1890. 2. Prisoners of war—United States—
Biography. 3. Dakota Indians—Kings and rulers—Biography.
4. Hunkpapa Indians—Kings and rulers—Biography. 5. Fort
Randall (S.D.)—Biography. I. Title.
E99.D1S6129 2010
978.004'9752—dc22
[B]   2010028845

Text and cover design by Rich Hendel

Please visit our website at www.sdshspress.com

Printed in the United States of America

14   13   12   11   10   1   2   3   4   5

To Deborah, Tony, Wallis, and Richard

CONTENTS

LIST OF ILLUSTRATIONS

PREFACE

Once upon a time, I was going to write a biography of Sitting Bull. Then I read Robert Utley's *Lance and the Shield* and gave up the idea. I felt there was no way I could improve on, or add anything new to, his book. However, there is a period in Sitting Bull's life that is usually skimmed over in all the biographies, and that is the chief's time as a prisoner of war at Fort Randall. His first authoritative biographer, Stanley Vestal (Walter Stanley Campbell), gave it five short paragraphs in his book *Sitting Bull, Champion of the Sioux*, but without Vestal's researches, all subsequent biographies would be skimpy indeed. Apparently, Vestal originally wrote a chapter on Sitting Bull's time at Fort Randall, but it never made it into the final draft. It does not even exist in the Campbell Archives at the University of Oklahoma. Robert Utley put things right by devoting a whole chapter to Sitting Bull's surrender and "imprisonment" at Fort Randall. Later, Jerome A. Greene in his book *Fort Randall on the Missouri* gave a good account of Sitting Bull's time at the fort. However, the overall scope of these books made it impossible for the authors to go into the minute details of Sitting Bull's surrender and imprisonment.

Sitting Bull's time as a prisoner of war was an important part of his life. It was the first time he had proper dealings with his old enemies, and he was no doubt as much surprised at his treatment as they were at the chief's behavior. During this time, Sitting Bull would learn how to deal with the white men who now controlled his life and his people. How he would adapt interested me, and initial researches led me to believe that there was a story here. Through the details of his time as a prisoner of war, the reader can learn much about the man himself, whether the facts or events be important or mundane. Details such as his wife Four Robes being heavily pregnant during the chaotic loading of the prisoners onto the *Sherman* and giving birth to a daughter during the journey down to Fort Randall put flesh on the bones of history.

This story has as much to do with Sitting Bull as with the soldiers and government officials who dealt with him. Distant officials in Washington did not have much respect or consideration for him, but those white men who had to deal with him face to face were generally sympathetic, kind, and considerate to their old enemy. This book is as much about the "ordinary" people he met—Alice Fletcher, Thomas Tibbles, Rudolf Cronau, Paul Boyton, Rev. John P. Williamson, and Bishop Martin Marty—as it is the story of Crazy Dog, White Dog, Strike-the-Ree, and little Gertie Bell. All played their part, albeit small, in Sitting Bull's life. They were, after all, real people whose stories deserve to be told.

SITTING BULL, PRISONER OF WAR

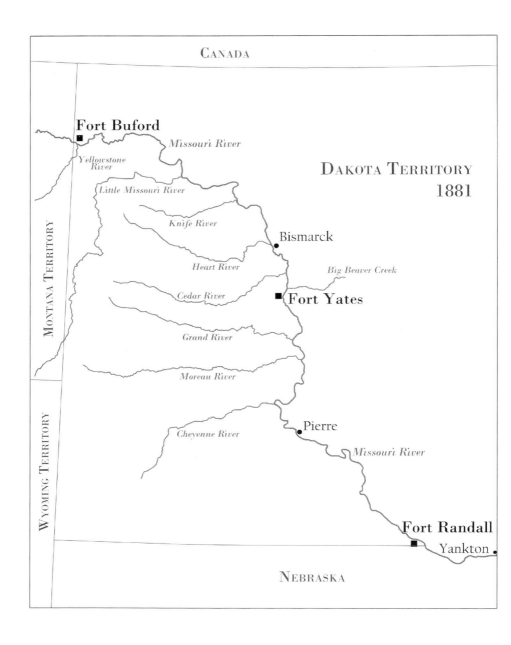

CANADA

Fort Buford

Missouri River

Yellowstone River

Little Missouri River

Knife River

Bismarck

Dakota Territory
1881

Big Beaver Creek

Heart River

Cedar River

Fort Yates

Montana Territory

Grand River

Moreau River

Cheyenne River

Pierre

Missouri River

Wyoming Territory

Fort Randall

Yankton

Nebraska

PROLOGUE

As the expansion of the United States pushed American Indian nations westward, the Sioux became part of the enforced western movement. One of the largest of the Indian nations, they were originally a confederacy of seven tribes: the Mdewakantons, Wahpetons, Wahpekutes, Sissetons, Yanktons, Yanktonais, and Tetons. The latter were also known as the Lakota, or Western Sioux, and were the first to cross the Missouri River and move out onto the Great Plains in the 1700s, eventually establishing themselves in a territory that covered large parts of what is today Kansas, Nebraska, Wyoming, Montana, and North and South Dakota. They acquired horses and quickly adapted to a nomadic life, becoming buffalo hunters and aggressive warriors. With the tribes they came in contact with, they were constantly at war. The Assiniboines, Crows, Flatheads, Blackfeet, Crees, Shoshonis, Poncas, and Pawnees were among their enemies, and all suffered from Lakota tribal and individual war parties and, of course, the inevitable horse-raiding expeditions. The war was not one way, though, as all these tribes also sent out war parties against the Lakotas. The sedentary tribes—the Mandans, Arickaras, and Hidatsas—who lived in permanent earth lodges and farmed were useful to the Lakotas, who traded with them for corn and other vegetables. The Lakotas would spend time bartering and socializing with these tribes but then revert to war, occasionally just after trading with them. But even with these tribes, the Lakotas did not have it all their own way, as these peoples also sent out war parties to attack them.

The Lakotas or Tetons consisted of seven bands—the Oglalas, Brulés, Minneconjous, Two Kettles, Sans Arcs, Sihasapas (Blackfeet), and the Hunkpapas. With such a large area to roam over, the Lakotas would inevitably split geographically into two factions, often referred to as northern and southern. The northern Lakotas consisted of the Hunkpapas, Sihasapas, and Sans Arcs. The southern Lakotas consisted of the Oglalas and Brulés. It was not a rigid split, and there was much interchange between the two groups. The Minneconjous and Two Kettles appear to have wavered between the northern and southern groupings. While the northern Lakotas did not have permanent allies, the southern Lakotas had strong alliances with both the Arapahoes and the Cheyennes.[1]

During the first half of the nineteenth century, the Lakotas' enemies were other Indians. The white men in Indian country were principally fur trappers and traders whom the Lakotas generally tolerated as benefiting their economy. It was not until the second half of the century that conflict with the white man occurred. The eastern Sioux, the Santees or Dakotas, were the first group to launch major attacks on the white settlements, prompted by the mismanagement of their affairs by government officials, resulting in the so-called Sioux, or Minnesota, Uprising of 1862 (now often called the Dakota Conflict) in which they massacred white settlers and pillaged the settlements in western Minnesota. The Lakotas had nothing to do with this conflict, but it was nevertheless to have a dramatic effect on their lifestyle. In the aftermath of the uprising, troops were sent into Lakota territory to find and punish those eastern Sioux who had escaped. These so-called Minnesota renegades were led by Inkpaduta, an aggressive leader with a deep hatred of the white man. While Hunkpapas and Sihasapas were out hunting, they came into contact with Inkpaduta's renegades in late July of 1863 and were persuaded to join them in attacking the troops who were pursuing them. Their first fight came at a place called Dead Buffalo Lake on 26 July. It is probably here that Sitting Bull, now a leading warrior among the Hunkpapas, had his first taste of fighting the white soldiers. Other fights occurred throughout the remainder of 1863, but with little success for the Sioux.[2]

The following year, 1864, the military decided that in order to protect settlers and miners traveling across Lakota lands, forts should be established to contain the activities of the hostiles. The forts were built alongside rivers so that steamboats could supply them. Fort Rice, which the northern Lakotas took particular objection to, was established on the Missouri just north of the present-day South Dakota border. The government also reinforced their attempts to subdue the hostile Lakotas, sending out military expeditions against them in 1864 and 1865. At the same time, another expedition was sent out to make peace treaties with these same Lakotas. The whole of the northern plains was now crisscrossed by troops searching for the Lakotas, either to fight them or to make peace with them. At this time, Sitting Bull's position changed from that of a noted warrior to a leader with influence beyond his own tribe. Attacks on the forts increased; both Fort Rice in 1865-1866 and Fort Buford (in northwestern Dakota Territory near its border with Montana), in 1866-1867 became prime targets for the angry Lakotas.[3]

In 1868, a peace commission was sent out to make a treaty with the Lakotas that would clearly define what territory the western Sioux would be allowed to occupy. They received an area created exclusively for the Lakotas called the Great Sioux Reservation, which comprised the area that is now western South Dakota. Sitting Bull did not attend this council at Fort Laramie, but he did send Gall, who signed the treaty without really understanding its meaning. He was not alone. For the next few years, from 1869 to 1871, the Lakotas remained fairly quiet, largely due to the fact that the unceded territories in Wyoming and Montana allowed them to exercise the freedom they required. By 1871, however, the railroads were making an appearance across the lands, threatening the migrations of the vast buffalo herds and affecting the major food supply of the Lakotas. In 1874, the Black Hills Expedition, led by Lieutenant Colonel George A. Custer, discovered gold in the Black Hills, creating a need to bring all the Lakotas onto reservations. Sitting Bull became the main critic of this policy, which would destroy the old free way of life that he had fought to retain. Finally, the government decided to force those Lakotas who had not agreed to come in, along with their Northern Cheyenne allies, onto reservations.[4]

On 1 February 1876, three columns went in pursuit of the roving bands. Although aware that troops were out looking for them, the Lakotas still held the annual Sun Dance, during which Sitting Bull, as a main participant, had fifty pieces of flesh cut off each arm, went into a trance, and had a vision in which he saw soldiers falling into their camp upside down (a sign of soldiers being killed). News that troops under the command of Brigadier General George Crook were in the vicinity prompted the Lakotas and Cheyennes to ride out to stop him, camping in a place called Greasy Grass, but known to the white men as the valley of the Little Bighorn River. The results of the Seventh Cavalry's encounter with this large encampment shocked the people of the United States and, for the Lakotas, heralded their journey from victory to the absolute destruction of the old Sioux way of life.[5]

After the battle, the large camp at the Little Bighorn split into two. Crazy Horse went south, eventually surrendering at Fort Robinson in Nebraska Territory, where he was later killed. Sitting Bull moved northwards to avoid the troops under Colonel Nelson A. Miles, Fifth Infantry, sent to bring him in. A fight at Cedar Creek on 20 October 1876 forced Sitting Bull's followers to move farther away. At Ash Creek, in the midst of winter, on 18 December 1876, troops under the command of First Lieutenant Frank D. Baldwin, Fifth Infantry, attacked his camp, forcing the Hunkpapas to flee in the freezing cold. In order to keep his one hundred thirty-five lodges containing about one thousand people together, Sitting Bull crossed the border into Canada at the beginning of May 1877.[6] The first hostile Lakotas to cross into Canada had done so in December 1876, and more continued to flee north until the refugees from Crazy Horse's Oglalas arrived in October 1877.

The Canadians were now playing host to about six hundred lodges containing four thousand people—Hunkpapas, Oglalas, Minneconjous, Sans Arcs, and Sihasapas. The government had already allowed over a thousand Santee Sioux to take refuge in their country after the Sioux Uprising in Minnesota, giving them a reservation at Portage La Prairie where they lived peacefully. The Lakotas were different. They did not consider themselves a defeated people, and they expected to continue living in their traditional nomadic lifestyle while in Canada. The authorities agreed to let them stay in the country as long as they did not cross back over the border with hostile intent. Like the Canadian tribes, such as the Blackfeet and Crees, the Lakotas would be allowed to cross the border temporarily to hunt the few remaining buffalo herds that roamed between the two countries. Inevitably, some of the Lakota hotheads defied their chiefs and caused trouble along the Yellowstone River and other areas close to the border, but United States troops under the command of Colonel Miles quickly sent the hunters fleeing back. Apart from these minor raids, the Lakotas did not commit a major hostile act.[7]

Although the presence of so many Lakotas could have created an explosive situation, the North West Mounted Police handled the situation well. Under the local command of Inspector James M. Walsh, they earned the trust and respect of the Lakota chiefs. Soon all Sitting Bull wanted was a reservation for his people in Canada. However, in 1880 the Canadian government's attitude hardened. With the buffalo herds now having virtually disappeared from the prairies, the government had to feed all the Lakota refugees. Another blow to Sitting Bull's hope of a reservation came when Inspector Walsh, who was sympathetic to Sitting Bull's cause, was replaced by Inspector Lief Newry Fitzroy Crozier, who was not sympathetic and told the Lakotas bluntly that there was no chance of a reservation. He pointed out that their continual refusal to surrender to the United States could only end in starvation because the Canadians were no longer prepared to feed them.

With no rations and little game to hunt, the Lakota coalition began to break up. Groups began to move south and accept the terms of surrender that the United States demanded—give up their arms, ammunition, and horses and accept life on a reservation. Sitting Bull had firmly rejected these terms earlier when a peace commission, headed by Brigadier General Alfred H. Terry, had been sent out in October 1877 to induce the Lakotas to surrender.[8] Now the chief was left with no alternative. Trader Jean Louis Legaré, respected and trusted by all Canadian Indians, as well as the Lakotas, succeeded where others had failed. On the evening of 11 July 1881, Sitting Bull and his followers joined Legaré's caravan of Lakotas who were going to Fort Buford to surrender. They were the last of the formerly hostile Lakotas to surrender, although a few did decide to remain in Canada. For Sitting Bull, it was the end, but also a new beginning. He would continue his fight for the well-being of his people, as he saw it, but now he would use words rather than guns.

SURRENDER AT FORT BUFORD

CHAPTER 1

Beneath a blue sky that seems to dominate the land-scape of the Dakotas are two lines of mounted cavalry. Each line faces the other on opposite sides of the parade ground. The troopers in their blue uniforms, with yellow piping, are mounted on sleek, well-groomed horses. The morning sunlight catches the glint of brass buttons and insignia. They look straight ahead. At the bottom end of these lines stands a group of high-ranking officers representing both the infantry and cavalry branches of the United States Army. They look between the lines of troopers, towards the flatland outside the fort, at a slow-moving column of Sioux braves, escorted by outriders of the United States Cavalry.

These Sioux are an imposing sight. Chiefs with eagle-feather war bonnets gently flapping in the breeze, their beaded buckskin shirts fringed with human hair. Behind them ride the braves, stripped to their breech cloths, eagle feathers erect on the back of their heads, bone breastplates on bronzed chests. All have their faces painted in red, yellow, white, and black war paint. Their horses are decorated with feathers and paint. They ride erect and proud. Lances, adorned with fur and feathers, point proudly up to the blue sky. Winchester rifles, wrapped in heavily fringed and beaded buckskin cases, rest in the crooks of their arms. Although they have come to surrender, they ride proudly because they are the last of the hostile Sioux to come in—five years after they had defeated troops of the Seventh Cavalry, under the command of Lieutenant Colonel George A. Custer, at the Little Bighorn.

Their leader dismounts. One of the officers steps forward to meet him. The chief walks towards him, his war bonnet's eagle-feather tail trailing on the ground behind him. The two *men look at each other. Both are proud of the rank they hold in their respective armies. Cautiously, hands are extended and then firmly shaken. This moment is one the army has long waited for—the surrender of the leader of all the hostile Sioux, Chief Sitting Bull.*

This scenario is how the moviemakers and the writers of western fiction would have portrayed the event. The reality was quite different. To begin with, the weather at Fort Buford on Tuesday, 19 July 1881, was dull and windy, with an overcast sky and occasional showers—no sunshine or blue sky. Just before noon, an air of excitement hung over the fort. A guard of six troopers mustered at the southwest corner of the parade ground. Groups of soldiers and civilians gathered outside Leighton and Jordan's post trading store on the west side of the parade ground. Opposite were the officer's quarters, where several officers had gathered with their families on their porches. In the pathways between these quarters, more civilians and off-duty soldiers had gathered. The commanding officer, Major David H. Brotherton, Seventh Infantry, stood outside the front of his office. All looked north, past the parade ground to the flatland outside the fort, watching the approach of columns of horsemen, both Lakota Sioux and soldiers. The gaunt ponies of the Lakotas contrasted with the groomed and well-fed horses of the cavalrymen who rode alongside them. Behind them came a procession of six wagons, loaded with women and children, followed by twenty-five to thirty Red River carts carrying their camp baggage. These carts emitted a screeching noise that could be heard from quite a distance away, adding to the melancholy of the occasion. Their six-foot wheels ran on ungreased axles that made ear-piercing noises that were likened to fingernails being scratched across a pane of glass, but much louder.[1]

The onlookers at the fort had seen similar processions before when the followers of Gall had surrendered on 10 January and when Crow King's people had surrendered on 5 February. At one time, well over a thousand Lakotas were camped around Fort Buford, all ex-hostiles who had returned from Canada where they had sought refuge after their victory at the Little Bighorn. As much as the people at the fort were used to seeing hungry and destitute prisoners of war, they now witnessed the entry into the fort of an even more forlorn group of 188 Lakota men, women, and children.[2] The effects of near starvation were clearly visible. Their clothing was falling apart from rottenness, and some had only dirty old blankets covering their half-naked bodies. These people were not surrendering because of defeat in battle. They were surrendering because they were starving and had nowhere else to go now that the Canadians were no longer prepared to feed the American Sioux.

The cause of excitement at Buford that day was the fact that the Lakota at the head of the procession, slowly riding alongside the Indian trader Jean Louis Legaré, was the most notorious Indian in the world—Sitting Bull. This day he did not look the part. What the onlookers saw was a man dressed in a dirty threadbare calico shirt, plain black leggings, and an old dirty woolen blanket wrapped around his waist. His face was partially hidden by a calico hand-kerchief, wrapped turban-like, around his head. This bandana was pulled low over his eyes to protect them from the light, as he was suffering from an eye infection, a condition he was prone to. His attire was among the shabbiest in that dismal procession of his own Hunkpapa Lakota band, *Itazipe Sica*, the "Bad Bows."[3]

Entering the fort, the procession passed the officer's quarters and Brotherton's office. Sitting Bull looked sullenly ahead, ignoring the watching officers on their porches and those onlookers, military and civilian, who walked alongside. At the end of the parade ground, the group turned right into a small camping ground behind the store-houses and the post gymnasium. Here Captain Walter Clifford, Seventh Infantry, who was in command of the escort, stopped the column and told the Hunkpapas to dismount and set up their camp. As the women busied themselves in unpacking the wagons and setting up their tipis, the men, as of old, sat around smoking and talking. Setting up camp was woman's work. The men did not interfere.

Major Brotherton walked across the parade ground to meet Sitting Bull. He shook the chief's hand and told him that his people could now prepare meals and rest for the remainder of the day. Sitting Bull asked to have a council with the major after he had eaten and rested, but Brotherton told him that they would talk the next day. For now, his people would have to give up their guns and horses, although at Sitting Bull's request the major permitted the chief to keep his Winchester until the council next day. The post adjutant, Second Lieutenant George S. Young, Seventh Infantry, and his guards

8

went around the camp, confiscating the Indians' horses and the few firearms and ammunition they had left. Although keeping his Winchester .44 caliber carbine, Sitting Bull had to give up his other gun, an old smooth-bore Northwest rifle. Also to be given up were his two horses.[4]

Even as the camp was being set up, the site was inundated with inquisitive onlookers. Irritated, Sitting Bull made it known he did not want to speak to anyone. Accordingly, the camp was put off limits, and guards were posted around it to ensure that the Hunkpapas were left alone to eat and rest up for the remainder of the day. A reporter from the *Saint Paul and Minneapolis Pioneer Press* had managed to visit Sitting Bull as soon as the tipis had been erected. He brought news that he had recently seen the chief's daughter, Many Horses, at Fort Yates and that she was well and happy. This news should have pleased her father, but Sitting Bull was still reluctant to believe the word of a white man. He did, however, agree to talk to the reporter once he had eaten and rested, but by then the camp was off limits. The unknown reporter had to wait for his interview.

Brotherton had already returned to his office, where he sent off two brief telegrams. The first was to the commanding officer of the Department of Dakota, Brigadier General Alfred H. Terry, at Fort Snelling. It was brief and to the point: "Sitting Bull and his followers surrendered to me at noon to-day." The other dispatch went to Crow King of the Hunkpapas and Low Dog of the Oglalas, both now at the Standing Rock Agency. They were ardent followers of Sitting Bull, and the military acted on the belief that if they knew their leader had surrendered they would not be inclined to give any further trouble.[5]

As darkness began to blacken Fort Buford, Sitting Bull, surrounded by wives, sons, and daughters, settled down for the night. Sleep would have been slow to come. Darkness may have lessened the soreness of his eyes, but thoughts of past, present, and future may have kept him awake. He was no stranger to Fort Buford. He had led attacks on the fort in the late sixties. In those days, the post had been new, built in 1866, and was a typical military fort of the period, enclosed in a stockade with blockhouses on the northeast and southwest corners from which the soldiers could fire on any attacker with impunity. These fixtures were now gone and the fort

9

less forbidding, but back then, the Lakotas had looked upon it as an intrusion upon their lands. They had almost continually kept the soldiers pinned down inside the fort. Sitting Bull's siege of Buford was every bit as intense as Red Cloud's at Forts Phil Kearny and C. F. Smith to the south during the same years. A few months after Buford had been built, the Lakotas took possession of the icehouse and sawmill just outside the fort on 23 and 24 December 1866. On the morning of the second day, Sitting Bull taunted the soldiers, loudly singing to them while beating time on a large circular saw he had commandeered.[6]

As he lay in his tipi, the chief now had to accept that those days were over. The soldiers had taken all his people's guns and horses, leaving them totally defenseless. His trusted lieutenants, Gall and Crow King, had already surrendered. He and his small band were on their own. One question that may have gnawed at his thoughts was, what is going to happen to us? He knew that his adopted brother, Jumping Bull, had been imprisoned and put in irons by Major Guido Ilges, Fifth Infantry. Even more disconcerting, some mischief-maker had told Sitting Bull that his daughter, Many Horses, who had surrendered with his adopted nephew Old Bull's people, had also been put in irons when she arrived at Fort Yates. If this was the treatment they had received, would it be the same for all his family? Captain Clifford had tried to convince him that Many Horses had never been put in irons and that she was well and happy at Fort Yates. He did not believe him. The number of white men he had come to trust could be counted on one hand. He had been treated fairly and considerately so far, but then no doubt Crazy Horse had felt the same, and look what happened to him.[7]

Sitting Bull's thoughts were not just of himself and his family, but of his band as well. This pattern had always been his way. The Hunkpapas now with him had proved to be his most loyal supporters. They had suffered much in accepting his leadership. He was honor-bound to look after them. As much as he detested the fact that the old free days were gone forever and that reservation life was now inevitable, he intended to look after his people in the best way possible. Would the whites let him? The question would be answered next day, but for now, all was uncertainty. Death, prison, or reservation life, which would it be?

The following morning brought another day of overcast sky and drizzly rain. Just before eleven o'clock, Captain Clifford arrived at the Hunkpapa camp to tell Sitting Bull that it was time for the council. The chiefs and headmen walked together across the parade ground towards the officer's quarters. Sitting Bull, accompanied by his favorite son, Crowfoot, led the way with thirty-two Lakota men following behind. He was dressed in the same shabby attire of the day before, even to the turban partially covering his eyes. Clifford escorted them to Major Brotherton's quarters, where they went into the parlor, one of the few rooms in the fort large enough to accommodate them all. Ready to greet them were a small group of soldiers and civilians. Representing the military were Major Brotherton, Captain Clifford, and Captain James M. Bell, Seventh Cavalry. Major Ilges was also present, having arrived at the fort that morning. Representing the Canadian government was Inspector Alexander A. Macdonnell. Resplendent in the scarlet tunic of the North West Mounted Police, he had ridden into Buford the night before. Jean Louis Legaré, the Wood Mountain trader who had fed and coaxed Sitting Bull into finally surrendering, was among the civilians present. Two other civilians in attendance were George Fleury (the post interpreter) and the unnamed reporter from the *Pioneer Press*. Sitting Bull shook hands with a number of them. Legaré and Macdonell he looked upon as friends, but he declined to shake hands with or even speak to Major Ilges, the man who had imprisoned Jumping Bull. The formalities over, Sitting Bull sat in a chair to the left of Major Brotherton and laid his Winchester carbine on the floor between his feet. He sat there silently.

The major opened the council, laying out the government's policy towards the Lakotas who had already surrendered and informing the new arrivals that they would soon be sent down to Fort Yates to be reunited with their kinsmen. As long as Sitting Bull's people behaved themselves, the soldiers would not harm them and would treat them well. As the major's words were translated into Lakota by Fleury, the Hunkpapas acknowledged them with grunts of approval. All, that is, except Sitting Bull, who remained silent.

Brotherton now beckoned to the chief to speak. Sitting Bull sat quietly for a full five minutes, an oratory ploy he often used, and then made a short speech to the Hunkpapas present, which unfortunately was not translated. He turned to Crowfoot and told him to pick up his Winchester and give it to the major. Looking at the officers, he started to speak:

> I surrender this rifle to you through my young son, whom I now desire to teach in this manner that he has become a friend of the Americans. I wish him to learn the habits of the whites and to be educated as their sons are educated. I wish it to be remembered that I was the last man of my tribe to surrender my rifle. This boy has given it to you, and he now wants to know how he is going to make a living. Whatever you have to give or whatever you have to say I would like to receive or hear now, for I don't wish to be kept in darkness longer. I have sent several messengers in here from time to time, but none of them have returned with news. The other chiefs, Crow King and Gall, have not wanted me to come, and I have never received good news from here. I now wish to be allowed to live this side of the line or the other, as I see fit. I wish to continue my old life of hunting, but would like to be allowed to trade on both sides of the line. This is my country, and I don't wish to be compelled to give it up. My heart was very sad at having to leave the great mother's country. She has been a friend to me, but I want my children to grow up in our native country, and I also wish to feel that I can visit two of my friends on the other side of the line, viz.: Maj. Walsh and Capt. McDonald [sic], whenever I wish, and would like to trade with Louis Legare, as he has always been a friend to me. I wish to have all my people live together upon one reservation of our own on the Little Missouri. I left several families at Wood Mountain and between there and Qu'Appelle. I have many people among the Yanktonais at Poplar creek, and I wish all [of] them and those who have gone to Standing Rock to be collected together upon one reservation. My people have many of them been bad. All are good now, that their arms and ponies have been taken from them. (Speaking to Maj. Brotherton):
>
> You own this ground with me and we must try and help each other. I do not wish to leave here until I get all the people I left behind and the Uncapapas now at Poplar creek. I would like to have my daughter, who is now at Fort Yates, sent up here to visit

me, as also eight men now there (mentioning their names), and I would like to know that Louis Legaré is to be rewarded for his services in bringing me and my people in here.[8]

Having finished his speech, the chief resumed his seat next to Brotherton. The major and the other officers must have been surprised by the tone of the speech. Here was this defeated leader of the hostile Sioux spelling out for them, in his own way, his terms of surrender. He was a proud man with the ego to suit. He still considered himself unconquered and not beholden to any white man at all. His demands were unrealistic, but not to him. They were always the same in the many subsequent interviews he gave. They were in essence the same demands that he would make to Major James McLaughlin, the Standing Rock agent, when he was released from Fort Randall twenty months later. He was consistent if nothing else.

In replying to Sitting Bull's speech, Brotherton told him that his daughter and the other chiefs could not be brought up from Fort Yates to see him. Addressing Legaré, he asked him if he would help bring in the remaining Hunkpapas in Canada. Legaré agreed. Turning back to Sitting Bull, the major again assured him that all his people were being well treated. Before officially closing the council, he informed the Hunkpapas that Captain Clifford would now escort them back to their camp and that on their way they would stop at the quartermaster's stores, where they would each be given a new army blanket.

Back at camp, those Hunkpapas not at the council were eager to know what was going to happen to them, but their leader could tell them little, other than the fact that they would be going to Fort Yates to rejoin the Lakotas there. At the council, nothing had been mentioned about their long-term future, mainly because Major Brotherton did not know anything either. The Indians must have felt apprehensive, but later in the day, an issue of blankets to the women and children and those men who had not attended the council lightened the mood. The Hunkpapas needed more than blankets, though. Brotherton telegraphed his superior, General Terry, applying for an allowance of three dollars per person to purchase clothing for Sitting Bull's band. This request went through various channels until it ended up at the Bureau of Indian Affairs, where an official said that, due to the financial support already given to the hostiles who had previously surrendered, they had no funds left. The War Department, therefore, would have to pay the sum of $825.91 for the extra clothing and other items that were purchased from Leighton and Jordan, the post traders at Fort Buford.[9]

The day after the council, Sitting Bull was no doubt pleased to see Jean Louis Legaré loading up his carts with supplies and starting on his journey to bring in the remaining Hunkpapas, about thirty-five families still in Canada and camped at Wood Mountain and Qu'Appelle. The remaining nine days the Lakotas spent at Buford were quiet. The Hunkpapas were still an attraction, and officers and their families and other residents of the fort visited them constantly. Some came from as far away as Fort Keogh and Bismarck. Many of these visitors genuinely befriended the Hunkpapas; others were more concerned with obtaining souvenirs. The souvenir traffic resulted in a steady sale of what few possessions the Indians had, everything from saddles to moccasins. With the money thus obtained, the men bought much needed items and luxuries for themselves and their families. Leighton and Jordan did a brisk business.

On Tuesday, 26 July, Major Brotherton received the orders to send Sitting Bull and his band down the Missouri River to Fort Yates, south of Bismarck and close to the present-day border of South Dakota. The fort watched over the Standing Rock Agency, the home of the Hunkpapa and Sihasapa Lakotas and the Upper Yanktonais. The stern-wheeler *General Sherman* was coming down from Coal Banks in Montana and was expected to arrive at Buford on Thursday evening. When he was told of the arrangement, Sitting Bull objected, saying that he wanted to wait at the fort until Legaré returned with the rest of his people. This desire could well have been a delaying tactic. Although he had received the kindest of treatment at Fort Buford, he still did not trust the whites. Would he receive the same treatment at Fort Yates? The thought of being put in irons and in prison still haunted him. If that fate was his future, what would happen to his family and his people if he were not there to look after their interests?

On the evening of Thursday, 28 July, many Hunkpapas probably went down to the riverbank to watch the arrival and docking of the

Sherman. They had seen these stern-wheelers before, having fired a few shots at them in the past, but they may not have expected to be passengers on one. After breakfast in the morning, the women started to pack up all their belongings and take down the tipis. As soon as that was completed, the soldiers escorted them down to the riverbank, where they boarded the boat in a good mood. The prospect of being reunited with relatives and friends contributed to a happy frame of mind. They were going home.

As the *Sherman* pulled away, Major Brotherton returned to his office to send off a telegram to General Terry in his usual brief style: "Steamer Sherman left here for Standing Rock at six forty-five A.M., with Sitting-Bull and one hundred and eighty seven of his people.—Sent an escort of seventy under command of Captain Clifford, seventh Infantry.—No trouble."[10]

JOURNEY TO
FORT YATES

On board the *Sherman*, the Lakotas shared the main deck with their individual baggage, folded tipi covers, tipi poles, and their military escort, all in one relatively small space. Captain Clifford, together with the correspondent of the *Saint Paul and Minneapolis Pioneer Press* and any other affluent white passengers, would have been assigned one of the few small cabins in the middle of the upper deck, directly above the main deck. The Lakotas were probably allowed to walk around the upper deck, where the toilets were situated at the stern end. Explaining how to use them must have been challenging, however. A single steep stairway at the bow of the boat gave access to the upper deck. Many of the Lakotas had difficulty in ascending these stairs, and some of them went up on their hands and knees.[1] Their difficulty with stairs would continue and would be evident on their third and last journey, when they eventually returned to the Standing Rock reservation.[2]

During the journey, the Lakotas, children included, were well behaved and caused no trouble. They probably quite enjoyed the novelty of river travel, their only previous experience having been in hide bull-boats, which were similar to the Welsh corracle in design and construction. Due to the shallow draft of the stern-wheelers, it was normal practice to moor them at night because the pilot could not see the condition of the Missouri's unstable riverbed in the dark. The first evening out, the captain moored the *Sherman* a short distance below Fort Stevenson, having traveled about one hundred fifty miles. Once the boat was secured, the Lakotas quickly disembarked, the women taking blankets and cooking utensils with them. On dry land, they busied themselves finding wood and soon had fires started and began cooking the evening meal. The men sat around the campfire smoking and talking. No doubt, the soldiers looking on thought of them as lazy. This pattern reflected how it had always been, though; the women were in charge of setting up camp. After the meal, some groups started to sing traditional songs until it was time to bed down for the night. The Hunkpapas slept on shore, under the stars, watched over by guards from their escort. At dawn, the women prepared breakfast, after which they all filed back on board the boat to continue their journey down-river.

The next stop was Bismarck, and the trip was quickly made. As the Hunkpapas approached the first white man's city they had ever seen,[3] the men climbed to the upper deck to get a better view. The citizens of Bismarck had come out in force. Crowding along the riverbank, they vied for a good look at the infamous Sitting Bull. If they expected some noble figure wearing a war bonnet and beaded buckskin scalp shirt, they were mightily disappointed. While the chiefs and headmen had donned their best finery, their leader remained the most poorly dressed of them all. He wore plain blue leggings, a dirty white shirt with three red stripes painted down each sleeve, and moccasins with little beadwork on them. He was bareheaded, with his hair in three braids. The two hanging over his chest were wrapped in red flannel, and the third, his scalp lock, hung down his back. His face and neck were streaked with red paint. To protect his still painful eyes, he wore green-tinted steel-rimmed goggles. The only ornaments he wore were two brass rings, one each on the little and second fingers of his left hand, and a cheap, lady's gutta-percha bracelet on his left wrist. In one hand, he carried his pipe bag, and in the other, a large hawk's-wing fan with which to cool himself on this hot Sunday of 31 July 1881.[4]

As soon as the boat was tied up, the Lakotas disembarked so that they could receive two-day's rations. They were grouped together in a square formation surrounded by their military escort. Here Sitting Bull and some of the other headmen were separated from the rest of the Hunkpapas and taken over to a railway train, where they were introduced to B. D. Vermilye, the personal secretary of the general manager of the Northern Pacific Railway, and Captain C. W. Batchelor, one of the principal owners of its Yellowstone Line. They told the chief that he would be attending a reception in his honor so that he could meet some of the leading citizens of Bismarck and that it would be followed by a meal. Sitting Bull was then invited to board the general manager's plush private railcar to make the short journey to Bismarck's most prestigious building, the Sheridan House, but the locomotive caught his attention, and he expressed an interest in seeing it move. Accordingly it was steamed up and moved a short distance. The chief shook his head and said he would rather walk—so much for trying to impress Sitting Bull. He did, however, agree to go in a three-seater army ambulance drawn by a team of four mules.

In the front seat of the ambulance sat Sitting Bull, Captain Batchelor, and the driver. Behind them sat the chief's sister Good Feather (Pretty Plume), his uncle Four Horns, White Dog, Scarlet Thunder, High-as-the-Clouds, and Bone Tomahawk. Also crammed in was the interpreter assigned to Sitting Bull, Edward H. Allison, together with Vermilye and one soldier guard. Seeing their leaders getting into the ambulance, the Hunkpapas began wailing and crying. Unsure of what was happening, they began to panic, the uppermost thought in their minds being that their chiefs were being taken away from them to be put in prison. The people were totally surrounded by soldiers, who menaced them with their rifles in order to maintain control. The situation had become tense. Seeing the commotion, Sitting Bull stood up in the ambulance and spoke to them in a loud voice. Whatever he said calmed them down, and there was no further demonstration as the ambulance drove off.

Sitting Bull and his party were driven uptown to the Sheridan House, outside of which several hundred people had gathered. Taking the party inside, Captain Batchelor invited them to go upstairs to the elaborate, carpeted, and cushioned parlor. Here they sat on chairs placed in a semicircle, with Sitting Bull in the center. The single guard stood immediately behind him. Taking out his pipe, the chief lit it and began to puff away. When not smoking, he fanned himself with his hawk's wing fan while he talked to Allison, who sat on his left. The other Hunkpapas talked amongst themselves. Occasionally some remark was made that caused them to smile or laugh out loud. These remarks were not translated or recorded, but it is safe to assume that they were derogatory to the white onlookers who had crowded into the parlor. Various people came forward to ask for

Sitting Bull's autograph, even Captain Batchelor. The reception now turned into an autograph session with the chief signing his name, deliberately and confidently. His friend, the trader Gus Heddrich, had taught him to write his name in English when he was in Canada.[5]

The party stayed at the Sheridan House for about half an hour, after which they went downstairs and got back into the army ambulance for the short journey to their next stop, the Merchants Hotel. As they drove through the streets of Bismarck, a crowd of all ages followed them from place to place. At the hotel, Captain Batchelor and Vermilye had arranged for the banquet. The owners of the hotel, a Mr. Marsh and Mr. Wakeman, had laid on a spread for their visitors, "served as it would be to the Queen of England," the *Bismarck Tribune* reported.[6] Outside every window in the dining room, crowds of people jostled each other to get a view of the proceedings. At the table, the Hunkpapas were greatly amused when Allison translated the menu for them. When the food came, they handled their knives and forks as if it were their normal way of eating. In fact, the Indian way of eating meat was to cram as much into the mouth as possible, cutting off what was left outside with a knife and chewing away. Who taught Sitting Bull's Hunkpapas how to use a knife and fork is not known, but they certainly could not have made a habit of using them. Sitting Bull ate slowly, stopping quite often to fan himself. The ice cream for dessert caused a sensation. The Hunkpapas could not understand how the whites could cook something so cold in such hot weather.

When it came time to leave, Sitting Bull presented Captain Batchelor with his pipe and Vermilye with a pair of goggles. Before leaving, the chief was asked to sign the register, which he did in his usual slow and deliberate manner. Outside, the Hunkpapas got back in the army ambulance and returned to the levee and their people. With the Lakotas gone, the remaining guests celebrated the success of the occasion with the uncorking of bottles of wine, which no doubt had been kept out of sight during the meal. Back at the levee, the Hunkpapas left behind were no doubt relieved to see their leaders return. The chief had been away for three long hours. During this time, his people had eaten a large portion of their two-day's rations—no ice cream for them. Having gone hungry for so long, they welcomed the simple fare.

A large throng of people watched as the band trooped back onto the *Sherman,* which had now been loaded with sixty-five tons of freight. On board were a select group of white people who had been invited to meet Bismarck's famous visitor. Among them were some of the officers, with their wives, from nearby Fort Abraham Lincoln. Also present were Mr. H. F. Douglas, the post trader at Fort Yates, and Colonel Clement A. Lounsberry, the editor of the *Bismarck Tribune*. Captain Clifford introduced the chief to each one, and with Allison interpreting, Sitting Bull answered their many questions. Among the ladies present was Miss Emma Bentley, who offered a fine California pear to the chief. Taking it, he cut off a piece with his knife, tasted it, and said he liked it. Ever the ladies' man, in appreciation of this gift, he took one of the brass rings off of his finger, gently placing it on one of the young lady's fingers and folding her hand over it.

He had a long conversation with Lulu Picotte Harmon. Her mother was Matilda Galpin, known to the Lakotas as Eagle Woman, and Sitting Bull had met her when she, with her second husband Charles, had acted as interpreters for Father Pierre Jean DeSmet when he visited Sitting Bull's camp in 1868. Her daughter Lulu had married First Lieutenant William Harmon, Thirty-sixth Infantry, who was now the post trader at Fort Abraham Lincoln, having resigned from the army in 1870.[7] Being part Hunkpapa on her mother's side, Lulu Harmon spoke Lakota fluently, and she and Sitting Bull chatted away on a one-to-one basis. For a time, she took over Allison's role as interpreter when it was noticed that Sitting Bull seemed more relaxed, his conversation often punctuated with arm gestures. With Mrs. Harmon at his side, he introduced his family, pointing out his twins, who were dressed in buffalo-calfskin jackets with the hair outside and wearing earrings made from telegraph wire. He said that some of the chiefs were going to see the president soon, and that he desired to have "his twin children be sent also, that they might see the ways of the white men and of the Great Father at his home." His pride in his family was evident, and he let it be known that he was overjoyed that he would soon be seeing his eldest daughter, Many Horses, who was at Fort Yates. The whole of this audience lasted about half an hour.[8]

At six o'clock, the boat cast off to the accompaniment of a band playing on the quayside. Sitting Bull went up to the upper deck to relax after the excitement of the day. Here, shortly after leaving Bismarck, Captain Clifford came to see him. He asked the chief to come with him to his cabin and meet with the reporter from the *Pioneer Press*. This gentleman had been present ever since the surrender at Fort Buford, eager for an interview but always being put off by Sitting Bull. Clifford explained that he had been telling the reporter about his part in the chief's surrender and wanted him to confirm that what he was saying was true. The two of them, accompanied by interpreters, made their way to Clifford's cabin. Inside, Sitting Bull was formally introduced to the reporter, who sat at a table in the forward part of the cabin. Sitting Bull voiced a low "how" and seated himself opposite this representative of the press. Taking his pipe out of its bag, he filled and lit it. With Clifford also puffing away on a Havana cigar, the cabin soon filled with tobacco smoke. The story Clifford had given the reporter was read out and interpreted to Sitting Bull, who acknowledged the correctness of the story with frequent grunts. He was then told that the journalist, through his newspaper, would tell the chief's story to white people from all over the country, far and near. Sitting Bull's reaction was to hang his head and slowly fan himself with a large palm-leaf fan. After a few minutes, he proclaimed that he could not speak now, as none of his people were present to see that he told the truth. Clifford accordingly sent out for some of the headmen to join them. After a short time, Four Horns, Shoot-the-Bear, and Bear-That-Looks-Like-Stand-and-Kill-Him joined the group.[9]

The newcomers shook hands with the reporter, sat around the table, and the pipe was passed around. When Sitting Bull was asked to speak again, he did so for about five minutes, saying that he still would not talk to the white man now, but he promised to speak to him when they reached Fort Yates and he had seen his people. At this point the interview ended, and the Lakotas left. Clifford assured the disappointed, and by now exasperated, reporter that this promise would be kept. He then went on to accuse the interpreters of interfering with the progress of the talk. While waiting for Sitting Bull's headmen to arrive, the interpreters had held a private conversation with the chief that was not translated. They now told Clifford that Sitting Bull had demanded money to be interviewed and that was the reason for the failure of this talk. At no time during the interpreted parts of the talk was money mentioned. It would have been in keeping with Sitting Bull's later practice to ask for a fee, but his official interpreter Edward H. ("Fish") Allison, one of the interpreters, could well have been hoping to make a few dollars for himself. Not for nothing did the Lakotas, referring to his slippery nature, call the man Fish.[10]

All this must have frustrated the reporter, but he appears to have been used to dealing with Indians. "Experience has demonstrated to your correspondent," he wrote the next day, "that the Indian cannot be driven or urged. He considers every subject carefully, and it takes longer to get one good, satisfactory interview with an Indian chief than it does to pump a column each from fifty white men. Such at least has been the experience of your correspondent with Sitting Bull."[11]

The boat traveled about ten miles downriver from Bismarck before stopping. As usual, the Hunkpapas disembarked to prepare their evening meal and settle down for the night. In the time before sleep overtook him, Sitting Bull must have mused on his reception at the first white man's town he had ever visited. At the start of the day, he had had no idea what to expect and some trepidation over the reception he might receive. He knew that he was regarded as the architect of the Custer Massacre to which the whites attached so much importance. To him, it had been just another fight with the soldiers, and in his mind, the Lakotas and the Northern Cheyennes had been in the right in protecting their women and children. The white men did not see it that way, though. Would they be in a vengeful mood? Surprisingly, he had been treated as a celebrity and someone of importance. It was obvious that the whites regarded him as the principal leader of the Lakotas, and they had treated him accordingly. The fanfare confirmed his own opinion of himself as the only true leader of the traditional Lakotas. It was an opinion he never lost, and one that would be confirmed in the years to come. It was, however, an opinion that some of the white men who had to deal with him later much abhorred.

SOJOURN AT STANDING ROCK

On the morning of Monday, 1 August, after breakfasting and dressing themselves in their best attire, the Lakotas boarded the *Sherman* for the last leg of their steamboat journey. The boat hummed with excitement as the people looked forward to being reunited with friends and relatives at Standing Rock. This agency, which replaced the earlier Grand River Agency created by the Fort Laramie Treaty of 1868, had been built in 1873 on the Great Sioux Reservation. In 1875, the army built a small nondescript military post to guard the agency. The fort and agency were adjacent to each other on the broad flatland that started on a ridge above the lowland at the edge of the Missouri River. After 1876, the post grew in size and importance and was renamed Fort Yates, after Captain George W. Yates, Seventh Cavalry, who was killed at the Little Bighorn. By the 1880s, it was a typical military fort of the Northern Great Plains, similar to Fort Buford. The Standing Rock Agency was on the north side of the fort and consisted of a mixture of buildings—offices, residents' houses, storehouses, trading post, council house, school, and church. The agency served the Hunkpapa and Sihasapa (Blackfeet) Lakotas and the Upper and Lower Yanktonais.[1]

As the *Sherman* approached Fort Yates at noon on that hot and sunny day, the Lakotas thronged the decks in order to catch a glimpse of their kinsmen. The chiefs and headmen lined the forward part of the upper deck. Sitting Bull stood impassively, second from the end of the line, again the least adorned of all the chiefs. A large crowd of Lakotas waited on the riverbank, and standing in front, with arms folded, was the impressive figure of Gall. A group of whites stood nearby. A line of soldiers, with fixed bayonets, kept everyone away from the water's edge, a sight that possibly alarmed the Lakotas on the boat. As the *Sherman* came nearer the landing, they searched the crowd for familiar faces, and greetings of "how" were shouted across the river. On the upper deck, one of the chiefs held aloft a yellow cloth, about three feet square, on which was an image of a deer. Above and below this figure were two parallel lines, and in each corner, vertical double crosses joined as one. With this emblem, which may have been a *wotawe* ("war charm") from Sitting Bull's medicine bag, flapping in the breeze, the Lakotas on the steamer began a mournful chant, punctuated with warlike yells.[2] As the steamer neared the riverbank, the chanting slowly died away to absolute silence.

Once the *Sherman* tied up, it took some time before the gangplank was lowered. As soon as it was secure, the first person to ascend it was Running Antelope, a one-time supporter of Sitting Bull but now a leading chief of the reservation Hunkpapas. He made his way to the upper deck. Approaching Sitting Bull from behind, he put his arm around him, pressed his cheek to the chief's, and said something in Lakota that was variably reported as "my son" or "my love."[3] Sitting Bull just stood staring to the front, seemingly oblivious to this greeting. Running Antelope now went to the end of the line of chiefs and headmen and began to shake hands with each one of them, greeting them, "how, how." Reaching Sitting Bull, he found him wiping away tears from his face with a large handkerchief.

Sitting Bull, his uncle Four Horns, and Running Antelope were now taken into one of the *Sherman*'s cabins, where they were introduced to some of the post officers, their wives, and other residents from Fort Yates and the agency. Some of them found it difficult to accept that this poorly clad Indian, who shook their hands and chatted to them, was in fact the supreme leader of the hostile Sioux, whose very name had spread terror along the frontier a few short years ago. As usual, the chief was asked for his autograph and he willingly obliged. For the ladies there was no charge, but the men had to pay anything from one to five dollars. This audience lasted about half an hour, after which Sitting Bull rejoined his people, who were now being marched down the gangplank in single file and counted as they filed off the boat.

Once ashore, they were assigned a place close to the river, where they seated themselves in a circle, women on the outside, men on the inside. Sitting Bull quietly smoked his pipe while their possessions were off-loaded. The recently surrendered Lakotas who had come to see him and his people were kept away, and realizing that they were not going to meet their relatives and friends that day, Gall and the others gradually wandered back to their own camp about three miles away. Sitting Bull's group was now moved back from the riverbank to flatland about half a mile away. Here the women put up their twenty-three tipis in a traditional camp circle. In the evening, Many Horses was brought over to see her father, and both wept with joy as they embraced each other. The news that she had left her husband and was returning to her father's tipi pleased him enormously.[4] For once the whites had not lied to him: his daughter was safe and well, as were all his followers who had surrendered earlier.

Early next morning, a wagon carrying the carcass of a recently killed ox was brought into the center of the camp. The meat was weighed and apportioned out to the individual families. It was soon cooked, but some could not wait and had started eating it raw. At about nine o'clock, a party of whites entered the camp, among them the *Pioneer Press* reporter who had come for his long-awaited interview. They found the camp quiet, with just a few men lazily walking around or sitting and sunning themselves in the morning sun. The only active person was an old woman, reputed to be the oldest person in the camp, who was leaning on a staff and walking up and down outside Sitting Bull's tipi uttering a sad wailing sound. Entering this tipi, the visitors shook hands with the men present, and the customary greetings of "how" were exchanged. All sat, Indian fashion, on the ground among the Hunkpapas. Those present for the interview were, from left to right of the tipi entrance, One Bull, Mrs. E. A. Henderson of Minneapolis, Mrs. Crosby of Bismarck, Mrs. T. Douglas of Fort Yates, Chief Rauber, Sitting Bull, his interpreter Allison, the *Pioneer Press* reporter, the agency interpreter Joe Primeau, Four Horns, the army's interpreter Phillip Wells, Bone Tomahawk, Captain George M. Downey of the Twenty-first Infantry, and the Bismarck photographer Orlando S. Goff. Quite a tipi full.[5]

The reporter described Sitting Bull's home as being constructed of "fourteen round poles about twenty feet high, stuck into the ground and coming together about three feet from the top, thus forming a cone about twelve feet in circumference and fifteen feet high in the center. The covering consisted of buffalo hides with the hair removed and sewed together and so placed around the poles so as to leave the customary entrance and open place for the egress of smoke. The poles and skins in the entire camp were smoky and greasy." Inside, the tepee was sparsely furnished with buffalo robes and army blankets. The ashes of a fire had entirely died out in the center of the teepee, and a few cooking utensils were heaped near the entrance. A medicine bag and pipe were "suspended from one of the poles in reach of the chieftain when in a sitting posture."[6]

After a pipe was passed around, Sitting Bull was told that the purpose of this talk was to enable him to tell his story to the American people in his own words, for which he would be paid ten dollars. In describing the chief's attitude during the talk, the reporter wrote: "Some questions the great chief would refuse to answer entirely. Others he would study over from five to ten minutes before making a reply, and still others he would partly answer and then wander back to some previous or wholly new question. Sometimes he would become animated and his face would brighten up. Then again he would sit moodily toying with his pipe, absentmindedly plucking with his tweezers at a stray whisker or eyebrow that in defiance of the Indian customs was trying to grow." Whenever he spoke, he addressed the interpreter Allison and "was very prolific with expressions and graceful gestures."

The translations that follow are most likely Allison's, as the reporter remarked that Allison had "a good English education" and "in translating clothed the ideas of Sitting Bull in the English rather that the Indian form of speech." The first question asked was, where was he born and when? Sitting Bull's reply was flippant: "I don't know where I was born and cannot remember. I know that I was born, though, or would not be here. I was born of a woman[.] I know this is a fact, because I exist."

He then turned to Four Horns, and the two men held a lengthy conversation, at the end of which Sitting Bull continued: "I was born near old Fort George, on Willow creek, below the mouth of the Cheyenne river. I am forty-four years old as near as I can tell, we count our years from the moons between great events. The event from which I date my birth is the year in which Thunder Hawks was born. I am as old as he. I have always been running around. Indians that remain on the same hunting-grounds all the time can remember years better."

Asked about his family, Sitting Bull replied that he had nine children, including two pairs of twins, and two wives living. At this point Captain Downey interrupted the proceedings with the comment that Sitting Bull was more fortunate than he was because he could not even get one wife. Sitting Bull laughed. To the question of which was his favorite wife, the chief answered that he thought of them equally but did think that if he had a white wife then she might be the favorite. Asked about the names of his wives, he raised the side of the tipi cover and called a woman over to him, but what he said to her was not interpreted. The whites present thought he was asking her their names, for when he turned back to his audience, he then gave the names of his wives as Was-Seen-By-The-Nation and The-One-That-Had-Four-Robes.

Asked if he was chief by inheritance or, if not, what deeds of bravery had earned him the title, he replied:

> My father and two uncles were chiefs. My father's name was The Jumping Bull. My uncle that is in the teepee is called Four-Horns and my other uncle was called Hunting-His-Lodge. My father was a very rich man and owned a great many good ponies in four colors. In ponies he took much pride. They were roan, white and grey. He had great numbers and I never wanted for a horse to ride. When I was ten years old I was famous as a hunter. My speciality was buffalo calves. (Here Bull indicated with his arms how he killed the buffalo.) I gave the calves I killed to the poor that had no horses. I was considered a good man. (Here Bull again counted on his fingers and joints.) My father died twenty-one years ago. For four years after I was ten years old I killed buffalo and fed his people, and thus became one of the fathers of the tribe. At the age of fourteen I killed an enemy, and began to make myself great in battle, and became a chief. . . . An Indian may be an inherited chief, but he has to make himself a chief by his bravery.

At this juncture, the reporter tried to coax Sitting Bull into telling more about his later life, but, being cautious, the chief would not go beyond the age of fourteen. He apparently had no wish to antagonize the whites with accounts of battles and horse raids against them.

When asked who, apart from himself, he considered to be the bravest Sioux chief, Sitting Bull paused, took a long puff on his pipe, passed it round, and at the same time toyed with a knife he had taken out of its sheath. Reflecting on his current position, he stated that when he came to Fort Buford he had had to give everything up. The soldiers had only allowed him to keep a blunt knife, which he now used to fix pipes. In answer to the original question, he said that their were five great chiefs of the Sioux before him: Four Horns, Loud Voiced Hawk, Scarlet Horn, Big Heart, and Running Antelope. All were now dead apart from his uncle and Running Antelope. The latter he considered to be a fool because he had lived with the whites for so long. Sitting Bull's statement caused the interpreters to tell the reporter in English that Sitting Bull was jealous of Running Antelope's new and favorable standing at the agency, something that Sitting Bull quickly denied. This interchange made clear the differing perspectives of those present. The interpreters praised Running Antelope for having "done more than any other chief to get the Indians to surrender," while Sitting Bull scorned the other chief's long affiliation with the whites. Sitting Bull corrected the interpreter (indicating that his English was much better than he let on), saying that he "had *no hatred or jealousy* [emphasis in original] in his heart when speaking of other chiefs."

Further questions relating to how he had come to surrender and what wrongs he had suffered at the hands of the government, Sitting Bull initially refused to answer, but he later relented. Speaking in what the reporter considered an excitable and rambling fashion, the chief said:

Already have I told my reasons. I was not raised to be an enemy of the white. These five chiefs that I have named were not enemies of the white man. The pale faces had things that we needed in order to hunt. We needed ammunition. Our interests were in peace. I never sold that much land. (Here Sitting Bull picked up with his thumb and forefinger a little of the pulverized dirt in the tent, and holding it up let it fall and blow away.) I never made or sold a treaty with the United States. I came in to claim my rights and the rights of my people. I was driven in force from my land and I now come back to claim it for my people. I never made war on the United States government. I never stood in the white man's country. I never committed any depredations in the white man's country. I never made the white man's heart bleed. The white man came on to my land and followed me. The white men made me fight for my hunting grounds. The white man made me kill him or he would kill my friends, my women and my children.

The reporter next broached the subject of the Custer fight, flattering the chief and telling him how much the whites admired his conduct. "You showed yourself to be a great chief," the reporter said, but the chief replied that a Great Spirit had governed the outcome of the battle not he. The reporter persisted, however, saying that the battle had been so well fought that many people thought he must be a white man. The chief's answer to that was:

I was not a white man, for the great spirit did not make me a white skin. I did not fight the white man's back. I came out and met him on the grass. When I say Running Antelope is a fool I mean he made treaties and allowed the white man to come in and occupy our land. Ever since that time there has been trouble. I do not want aid or assistance from the whites or anyone else. I want them to stay from my country and allow me to hunt on my own land. I want no blood spilled in my land except the blood of the buffalo. I want to hunt and trade for many moons. You have asked me to come in. I wanted the white man to provide for me for several years if I came in. You have never offered me any inducements to come in. I did not want to come. My friends that come got soap and ax handles, but not enough to eat. I have come in, and want the white man to allow me to hunt in my own country. That is the way I live. I want to keep my ponies. I can't hunt without ponies. The buffalo runs fast. The white man wanted me to give up everything.

This response prompted the reporter to ask Sitting Bull what he expected of the government. The chief replied that he wanted the gov- 29 ernment to let him occupy his hunting grounds, "from the badlands to the end of the Little Missouri" and down to Fort Yates where some of his people were so that he would be able to trade. He wanted payment from the government for taking this land and the game on it.

After a few incidental questions, the reporter returned to the Custer battle, asking several questions to which the chief, after a long silence, replied: "I am not afraid to talk about that. It all happened, it is passed and gone. I do not lie, but do not want to talk about it. Low Dog says I can't fight until some one lends me a heart. Gall says my heart is no bigger than that (placing one forefinger at the base of the nail of another finger). We have all fought hard. We did not know Custer. When we saw him we threw up our hands and I cried, 'Follow me and do as I do.' We whipped each other's horses, and it was all over." He stated that there were not as many Indians in the fight as white men said—not more than two thousand. As to Crow King's report that on the second day, when they were fighting Reno's men, Sitting Bull had asked the warriors to call off the battle because enough soldiers had been killed, he replied: "Crow King speaks the truth: I did not want to kill any more men. I did not like that kind of work. I only defended my camp. When we had killed enough, that was all that was necessary." Those were Sitting Bull's last words on the subject, and nothing could be done to get him to go into more detail.

Changing the subject, the reporter asked if the chief had ever been interviewed before. In answering this question, he went on to state his demands for the future:

> I have never talked about these things to a reporter before. None of them ever before paid me money. My words are worth dollars. If the great father gives me a reservation, I do not want to be confined to any part of it. I want no restraint. I will keep on the reservation, but want to go where I please. I don't want a white man over me. I don't want an agent. I want to have the white man with me but not to be my chief. I ask this because I want to do right by my people and can't trust any one else to trade with them or talk to them. I want interpreters to talk to the white man for me and transact my business, but I want it to be seen and known that I have my rights. I want my people to have light wag-

ons to work with. They do not know how to handle heavy wagons with cattle. We want light wagons and ponies. I don't want to give up game as long as there is any game. I will be half civilized till the game is gone. Then I will be all civilized. I want peace and no trouble. I want to raise my children, that they may have peace and prosperity. I like the way the white brother keeps his children. Miss Fanny Culbertson of Poplar River was the first person I shook hands with when I came over the line. My daughter came to see me last night. We both cried. I was happy to see her. The soldiers would not let her come into my camp at first. She came here before I did, and I listened a long time to hear word from her, and for the winds to tell me how she was treated. I did not hear. I came down to see her. She seems to be doing well, but I saw she had no respect from the whites. The soldiers would not spread down a blanket for her to walk into my camp. She is well dressed, but she says her relatives at the Agency gave her clothes.

Going to an entirely new topic, the reporter had the interpreters tell Sitting Bull about the recent shooting of President James A. Garfield in July 1881.[7] What did the chief think about such an act, and what would the Lakotas do to a coward who killed a chief? Sitting Bull's reply was remarkably blunt:

It was a cowardly act. If the warrior had been there he would have gone to the Great Father's face and looked him in the eyes and then shot him. I heard when way up there [in Canada] about the Great Father being shot, but had no one to tell me all about it. I don't know whether the warrior was wise in doing it or not. He might have shot the Great Father because he was not treating the Indians right. If that was so it was not a bad thing to do. If a coward should shoot one of our chiefs or warriors without looking him in the eyes, our friends would go and kill him. If he was a very rich coward he could pay the damages in many ponies and we would let him leave.

To the next question of how many scalps had he taken, Sitting Bull thought for a full five minutes before stating that he had killed sixteen enemies. He had made raids upon the Crees, Gros Ventres, and Blackfeet. He had never killed a white man nor stolen horses from the whites. In this instance, he was bending the truth. According to his pictographic war record, made about 1870, he had killed one white man, counted coup on fifteen, and stolen horses from them on six occasions.[8] He was hardly going to mention these feats now that he was totally in the hands of the white man, however.

As the interview ended, the reporter told Sitting Bull that the president would be reading the words that he had spoken and asked if the chief had a message for him. "I have told you all I want," Sitting Bull replied. "I would like to have the Great Father listen to what I have said and help me accomplish what I ask."

The interview had lasted from 10:00 A.M. to 1:30 P.M. The pipe was passed around again, and the visitors, with handshakes and the usual "hows," left the tipi. The reporter was well satisfied, having at last gotten the interview he had patiently waited for. Photographer Goff was not so lucky; Sitting Bull postponed his appointment to have his photograph taken that afternoon. He did later have a sitting with Goff, who took at least two portraits, one of them with the chief wearing green-tinted steel-rimmed goggles. Sitting Bull did not like the photographs because his pale face made him look like a white man.[9]

On his arrival at Fort Yates, Sitting Bull had secretly received an invitation to visit the main ex-hostile camp for a council with the other chiefs, and he was eager to go. He wanted to know what had happened to those who had surrendered with Gall and Crow King, and they wanted to know what had happened to him. Canceling his sittings with the photographer, he now made his way over to the main camp, walking the three miles alone. Suspecting that he might not be given permission for such a visit, he did not bother to ask. There must have been some feasting, but the council between Sitting Bull and his lieutenants would have been the main priority in the *tiyotipi*. He stayed overnight, and sentinels were placed at various high points between the camp and Fort Yates to watch for intruders, or troops, that might be coming to take their leader back.[10]

In the afternoon of the following day, Wednesday, 3 August, the Lakota sentinels signaled to the camp with mirrors in a pre-arranged code that indicated that white men were approaching. At this moment, Sitting Bull made himself scarce in another part of the camp.

The whites approaching were the Standing Rock agent, Father Joseph A. Stephan, the intrepid *Pioneer Press* reporter, and two ladies, who sat on the back seat of the carriage. The reporter described the camp,

> which, upon close inspection after arrival proved to be very cleanly [*sic*], which, however, was due to the fact that it was a new camping ground and had been occupied but a few days. Among the several hundred tepees were three from the apex of which a small red flag floated, indicating that there was sickness within. The larger tepees here and there were occupied by the chiefs, and an unusually large one was used as a dance house. Hanging about on poles was the two weeks' supply of fresh meat, which had in some manner been cut into sheets nearly as thin as a piece of ordinary wrapping paper, and which was drying in the sun. Numerous poles [were] stuck into the ground, with peculiar and mysterious-looking packages suspended from the upper end, each package of which contained some root or herb. . . . A tepee of buffalo hide ornamented on the exterior with rude attempts at an artistic representation in paint of horses, Indian hunters, buffalo, deer, etc, was the habitation of noted warriors not yet having obtained influence, dignity or scalps to entitle them to enter the council of the chiefs. Grazing at a distance on the sides of the buttes were a number of ponies. . . . About three miles distant, on the brow of a hill, were outlined against the sky the poles upon which the dead bodies of departed spirits were suspended in a reclining position.[11]

The white visitors found the camp quiet, with men wearing nothing but moccasins and breechcloths eating bread and beans or just basking in the sunshine. The only activity they witnessed occurred on the outskirts of the camp, where a group of twenty-five to thirty men and women were excitedly gambling beads, moccasins, clothing, and other personal adornments on the turn of a card from several packs of playing cards. The visitors drove into the camp and stopped outside the *tiyotipi*, where Father Stephan and the reporter stepped down from the carriage and went inside. There they found about a dozen chiefs and headmen seated in a circle, engaged in a council that stopped immediately when they entered. What conversation followed was not recorded, apart from the fact that Father Stephan was concerned about an auburn scalp attached to the top of one of the lodge poles outside and gently swaying in the breeze. He may well have asked for it to be taken down, but the only reply he received was the information that Running Antelope had a buckskin shirt decorated with the scalps of white men and women. So what was the difference? A few of the men went outside to be introduced to the two ladies, greeting them with the usual "how" and a handshake, but Gall insisted that the ladies remove their gloves before he would shake their hands. As for Sitting Bull, there was no sign of him. Father Stephan was sure he was there but did not press the point. No doubt that evening, under cover of darkness, the chief made his way back to his own camp.[12]

Throughout most of August, Sitting Bull's camp remained quiet. While the women could continue with their usual lifestyle, the men, now denied the hunt and the warpath, had little to do. They passed the time in gambling or just sitting around smoking and reminiscing about the past. For the children, life was more or less the same as of old, except that the boys had no ponies to ride or look after. Visits between the two Lakota camps offered some diversion, and social occasions, such as dances and feasts, still took place. For Sitting Bull, a visit from Mrs. Galpin, known to him as Eagle Woman, relieved some boredom. This extraordinary woman, the daughter of a Two Kettle father and a Hunkpapa mother, had accompanied Father Pierre Jean DeSmet, as interpreter, when he had visited Sitting Bull's camp on behalf of the peace commission in 1868. It was only natural that she should wish to visit the chief now. She was sympathetic to his position, and the two had several discussions about the future of his people. Although they had opposing views on what that future should be, a genuine friendship grew up between them, both respecting each other's opinions.[13]

When the Lakotas had returned to Dakota Territory from Canada, another local inhabitant had also returned—the buffalo. The *Pioneer Press* of 15 August 1881, reported a herd of seventy-five thousand buffalo within forty miles of Standing Rock, causing great excitement among the Lakotas. With the buffalo now so close, the Indians were anxious to go out and hunt them, but they had to have permission from their agent, who could assign passes at his own discretion. There was no way that all the formerly hostile Lakotas could be allowed to go out en masse, but small parties were permitted.

On the morning of 24 August, a party of 150 men left the agency to hunt buffalo in the Little Missouri region, about 125 miles away. Because of differences between Father Stephan and Lieutenant Colonel William P. Carlin, Seventeenth Infantry, the post commander at Fort Yates, it is possible that the military were not informed of this hunting party. It is equally possible that the Lakotas went off without asking permission. It was always difficult for the chiefs to control their young men. Whatever the case, as soon as the military were aware of the situation, they sent small detachments of troops from both forts Yates and Abraham Lincoln to head off the Lakotas and return them to Standing Rock, pass or no pass.[14] The hunting party did not come from Sitting Bull's camp. He was too closely watched, and the military would not give him a horse and gun to go roaming around the country. The fact that a group of hunters could be first given permission to hunt and then have it taken away only deepened Sitting Bull's mistrust of the white man, however. The Indians' freedom was gone, and the situation would have rankled the chief, who had clearly stated that he wanted no white man telling him when and where to hunt.

On 23 August, the day before the hunters left on their abortive effort, Sitting Bull had experienced another instance of the control the white man now had over his people. Soldiers had discovered, and immediately confiscated, some shotgun cartridges found in his camp. While there is no report of what followed, it is safe to assume that the finding resulted in a thorough search. The disruption as soldiers searched every tipi, its contents, and maybe individuals, with military thoroughness and insensitivity, would have alarmed the powerless Hunkpapas who could do nothing but watch. Their major concern at this time must still have been what was going to happen to them. In spite of promises made, there had as yet been no attempt to settle them on a reservation. Towards the end of August, Sitting Bull went to Father Stephan to ask for a plot of land on which he could start farming, but nothing came of his request. In fairness to Stephan, he had no authority over Sitting Bull and his band. Their future lay in the hands of the military, and they were dithering.[15]

35

Rumors were rife among Sitting Bull's band as to their future. One story, probably instigated by Allison, was that they were to be sent to the Indian Territory in Oklahoma. Sitting Bull told a reporter that he did not believe the government would send him there and was not inclined to react until he had official confirmation. Some whites voiced the opinion that the land there was better suited to farming than in Dakota Territory. The Indians who had already gone there did not agree. After surrendering in 1877, a third of the Northern Cheyennes under Dull Knife and Little Wolf had been set to Fort Reno in Indian Territory, where they suffered much from illness and death. The following year, they broke out and made their epic return to their old hunting grounds in Montana. This story was known to the Lakotas, who reasoned that, if the Cheyennes did not like it there, then they would not either.[16]

Even as rumors flew, the military continued to show that they were in total control of the Lakotas. Sitting Bull's camp housed two families of Minneconjous from the band of Chief Hump, and he wanted them back with him. On 31 August, he came and took them and all their belongings back to his camp. It is doubtful that he could have managed the removal without Sitting Bull's agreement. As soon as the military learned of it, they intervened, and on 1 September, the two families were returned to Sitting Bull's camp as prisoners of war. Also, at about this time, one of Sitting Bull's Hunkpapas was in trouble with the military for selling his tipi and other government-supplied property. What the white man gave them they had to keep—something else the Indians would now have to get used to.[17]

When Sitting Bull surrendered, he had been a defeated man, one with no hope and quite possibly dreading the future—for himself and his followers. But this situation had begun to change. Being feted at Bismarck and interviewed like a celebrity in the shadow of Fort Yates was not what he had expected. He now sensed that the whites regarded him as an important leader of the Lakotas. His initial humble attitude changed as the press continued to interview and follow him. Even as the military continued to circumscribe his movements, Sitting Bull could see the possibility of starting a new way of life on his own terms, making demands that would secure a future for his people and himself as leader.

REMOVAL TO FORT RANDALL

Although it was over one month since Sitting Bull's surrender, he still had no indication of the future disposition of his band. Unbeknown to the chief, and to the personnel at the agency and the fort as well, his future had already been decided far away. The secretary of the interior, Samuel J. Kirkwood, and the secretary of war, Robert T. Lincoln, had come to the conclusion that with so many formerly hostile Lakotas gathered in one place, namely Standing Rock Agency, the presence of their leader could lead to trouble, given the "malign influence of Sitting Bull."[1] In spite of what formerly hostile leaders like Gall and Low Dog said, often for the benefit of their own reputations, the recently surrendered bands still regarded Sitting Bull as their principal leader. In mid-August, the reporter for the *Saint Paul and Minneapolis Pioneer Press* interviewed George R. Sage, a prominent member of the Cincinnati bar who had spent much time at the agency. Sage told the reporter that chiefs from the different agencies were visiting and counseling with Sitting Bull. Adding that he himself was much impressed with the chief, he noted that he had seen him, "time and again sitting as center of a ring of chiefs—Gall and others, who before his coming made light of his authority and pretensions—and talking to them so friendly and evidently, even to me who did not understand their language, so well that the strictest attention was paid him."[2]

The military would have noticed this respect and reported it back to Washington. On 22 August, the adjutant general of the army, Brigadier General Richard C. Drum, sent a telegram to the commanding general of the Military Division of the Missouri, Lieutenant General Philip H.

37

Sheridan, which read: "In accordance with instructions from the [secretary] of war, the General of the Army directs that you instruct General Terry to order the removal from Fort Yates to Fort Randall of Sitting Bull & the Indians who recently surrendered with him & to hold & provide for this Band of Indians at Fort Randall as prisoners of war till further orders."[3] The military now sprang into action. The following day, 23 August, the commanding officer of the Department of Dakota, Brigadier General Alfred H. Terry, advised Drum that the transfer of Sitting Bull would have to wait for the stern-wheeler *General Sherman* to come down from Rocky Point, via Forts Buford and Yates, and that this would take several days.

Not everyone was happy about the removal of Sitting Bull. The *Bismarck Tribune* of 2 September was somewhat prophetic:

The war department will find that a mistake has been made in ordering the removal of Sitting Bull to Fort Randall. It was only necessary to strengthen the garrisons at Fort Yates and Fort A. Lincoln[,] making a display of force, to keep these Indians in subjection. To divide them and send off a portion as prisoners of war will create uneasiness and probably lead to trouble. If it was intended to punish them it would be different, but it is only intended to dally along with them and in the end send them back to their tribe or at least place them on a separate reservation.[4]

Major James McLaughlin, due to take up his new post as the agent at Standing Rock, voiced the same opinion in a telegram to the commissioner of Indian affairs in which he said, "I regard it very unwise, it will create disturbance and affect the others."[5]

On 1 September, the order for Sitting Bull and his band's removal was telegraphed to the commanding officer at Fort Yates, Colonel Charles C. Gilbert, Seventeenth Infantry, from the assistant adjutant general, Department of Dakota, Major Samuel Breck, informing him that in three or four days the *Sherman* would arrive at the fort to take the prisoners of war to Fort Randall. He stressed the fact that no other boat should be used. On board would be G troop of the Seventeenth Infantry for temporary attachment to the garrison, while one company from Fort Yates would accompany the prisoners on their journey, "under a most careful and experienced officer," and that they were to return on the *Sherman* after handing over their charges. The final sentence read, "Do you anticipate any trouble in the move, or any need for more troops?"[6] Gilbert replied on the following day that he did not anticipate trouble. He advised that he had no immediate need for extra troops but added that he would like to receive new recruits to increase his small companies, which were "objects of ridicule."[7]

Although Gilbert had received his orders on Thursday, 1 September, it was not until the evening of Tuesday, 6 September, that he informed Sitting Bull of the pending removal to Fort Randall. Wisdom had probably prompted this delay. Knowing the trouble this order could cause, the officer judiciously postponed telling the chief until the arrival of the *Sherman* was only a few days away. When told, Sitting Bull was furious. The *Bismarck Tribune* reported that Sitting Bull "protested against the removal, and carried on at a great rate during the night." The soldiers would have to kill him before he would go, like they had Crazy Horse, Sitting Bull reportedly said. He was angry with everyone. After all, the Black Robe—Abbot Martin—had lied to him. The Redcoats had lied to him. As for Allison, the chief swore he would kill him next time he saw him.[8] All along, the white men had lied to him. In Canada, General Terry had promised him a full pardon and told him, "no attempt will be made to punish you or any of your people; what is past shall be forgotten and you will be received in as friendly terms as other Indians have been received."[9] At Buford, he had been told that he was going to the Standing Rock Agency where he would be reunited with his people and, as long as he and his band behaved themselves, they would not be harmed. All lies! The fact that no one would tell him what was actually going to happen to him when he arrived at Fort Randall gave him black thoughts—as much for himself as for his people. Would they all be put in chains and locked up in a prison? Would they, like many of the Santee Dakotas who surrendered after the Minnesota uprising, be put on trial and hung?[10]

The following morning, Sitting Bull had calmed down a little and asked for a council with Colonel Gilbert. His request was refused, which only stoked his anger and frustration. Gilbert had no doubt anticipated this reaction and the effect it could have on the main hostile camp. In a move that was probably preplanned, and not entirely due to Sitting Bull's outbursts, Company H, Seventeenth Infantry, under command of Captain Henry S. Howe, supported by Company D of the Seventh Cavalry, was sent to the chief's camp to order it to be taken down and moved back to the riverbank where his people had landed when they first came to Fort Yates. Here the military were better placed to watch over the Hunkpapas and prevent any escape. In any case, the Hunkpapas would have to be moved to the river before the estimated time of arrival of the *Sherman* in order to be ready for immediate embarkation. The military also worried about the close proximity of the main hostile camp and the murmurs of discontent that chiefs such as Gall and Crow King were uttering over the removal of their leader; a major outbreak appeared to be a distinct possibility. The fort's artillery was readied for instant use; the infantry were put on full alert; the cavalry's horses were saddled ready to be mounted at a moment's notice; and all personnel, military and civilian, were armed.[11]

The next few days were tense. The Hunkpapas, unable to offer any outright resistance, appeared to calm down. Perhaps Sitting Bull was hoping that a letter he had sent to the Bureau of Indian Affairs saying that he was satisfied with his treatment at Standing Rock and wanted to stay there would win a last minute reprieve.[12] It was not to be so. His letter did not reach Washington until 7 September, too late to change anything, and in any case, he had sent it to the wrong people—the Indian Bureau was not in charge of him. The War Department controlled his future.

On Saturday morning, 10 September, at eleven o'clock, the *Sherman* arrived at Fort Yates. Sitting Bull and his people reacted with anger and despair at the sight of the boat. The order soon came for the camp to be taken down and all belongings packed, under the watchful eyes of two companies of infantry and two companies of cavalry. Resistance would have been futile—forty unarmed men against all those soldiers. The Hunkpapas were powerless. One woman was so distraught that she took a knife and killed her child, but before she could turn the knife on herself, she was overpowered and the weapon taken away from her.[13] Her actions speak to the state of dread prevalent among the Hunkpapas at this time.

As soon as the passengers and soldiers on board the *Sherman* had disembarked, the soldiers surrounding the Hunkpapas acted. With fixed bayonets, they formed a skirmish line, gradually pushing the Indians into a tight mass, shoulder to shoulder. The men were angry, the women and children frightened. The men did their best to keep their families together. At least one woman had flown into a panic because her husband was not with her, but there was no one to translate her words.[14] Men whose wives were not with them were equally upset. Sitting Bull had his hands full in shielding and comforting the younger members of his family. His mother (Her-Holy-Door), both his wives (the heavily pregnant Four Robes and Seen-by-the-Nation), his teenage daughters (Many Horses and Sun-While-Walking), his fifteen-year-old son (Stood-by-Him), and his mother-in-law (Lost Woman) all helped him to protect the young girls (five-year-old Her-Lodge-in-Sight and four-year-old Stands Holy) and the young boys (seven-year-old Crowfoot, the three-year-old twins On-the-Hill and Left-Him, and his stepsons Blue Turtle and Little Soldier). The soldiers pushed and prodded the tightly packed Hunkpapas toward the gangplank and forced them up it and onto the boat. Sitting Bull's nephew and adopted son, One Bull, had to be shoved on board with the butt of a rifle. Stories that Sitting Bull was either knocked out or bound hand and foot in order to get him on board are likely untrue.[15]

One of the passengers disembarking that day was Major James McLaughlin, the new agent at Standing Rock. Learning of his presence, Sitting Bull asked to see him. As soon as the major had seen that all his goods had been put ashore, he went back on board to meet the chief. Sitting Bull recited his grievances about his removal from the agency. Perhaps the chief hoped that at the last minute the new agent would rescind the order for his removal. Although McLaughlin was not in favor of removing Sitting Bull, he was powerless to act. Their first meeting was brief but friendly and polite. When the two men parted, both probably thought that they could work together in the future, but they were individuals of the same temperament with different ideals. They were destined to be nearly always at loggerheads.[16]

At half past two, the *Sherman* cast off. The Hunkpapas must have looked a forlorn sight as they watched Fort Yates slowly disappear from sight. The presence of their escort, Company H under Captain Howe, indicated to them that they were still prisoners of war—

prisoners with an uncertain future. The four-hundred-mile journey down the Missouri to Fort Randall took a week. It was a quiet trip. Although they passed Pierre and other towns, the military permitted no stopovers at which Sitting Bull could be feted by a curious populace. The only recorded event occurred when the boat passed the Cheyenne River Agency at Fort Bennett, where a large group of Lakotas had assembled on the riverbanks. As the boat passed, "the most violent demonstrations of grief occurred," one newspaper reported. A few days before, 120 ex-hostiles from Standing Rock Agency, under the leadership of Spotted Eagle and Two Eagles, had been transferred to the Cheyenne River Agency, and their presence was having an unsettling effect. The agent, Major Leonard Love, was concerned that Sitting Bull's influence would be extended to his Lakotas by the presence of these followers of the chief. The demonstration on the riverbanks was an indication of the regard and concern that the Lakotas still held for their old leader.[17]

Sitting Bull's journey continued in the same pattern as before, however. Each night, the Hunkpapas disembarked to prepare their evening meal and sleep under the watchful eyes of their guards. During the day, they had little to do but watch the countryside slip by and sit around smoking and talking. There was one bright spot for Sitting Bull. During the first day or night of the journey, Four Robes gave birth to a baby girl. Always the proud father, he would have spent much time with her before their arrival at the fort.[18]

Fort Randall had been established in 1856 with the principal duties of the troops stationed there being to maintain peace among the Indians in the vicinity—the Brulé Lakotas, the Yanktons, and the Poncas—as well as providing escorts for mail and supply trains from Sioux City, Iowa. The fort served as a base for any proposed military expeditions. In the 1870s, troops from the fort had been called upon to stop illegal gold prospectors from going to the Black Hills and to protect surveyors of the Northern Pacific Railway. Troops from the fort also took part in the Yellowstone expeditions of 1871, 1872, and 1873. During these times, the fort itself was used principally as a depot for supplies. Unlike Forts Rice and Buford, Fort Randall did not come under major attacks from the northern Lakotas, being outside of their territory. In fact, the garrison had few confrontations with local tribes. Over the years, buildings had deteriorated and new ones had been built. By the time Sitting Bull arrived, Fort Randall had taken on the appearance of an open fort with a central parade ground surrounded by barracks and officer's quarters. It did have one distinctive feature—a stone chapel built in 1875.[19]

The *Sherman* arrived at Fort Randall in the evening of Saturday, 17 September. There was not much time for formalities, and the Lakotas were told to pitch their camp next to the fort. After their evening meal, they settled down for the night, wondering what was going to happen next day. On the morning of 18 September 1881, Captain Howe officially handed over his prisoners to Colonel George L. Andrews, Twenty-fifth Infantry, the commanding officer at Fort Randall. Four separate officers counted the new charges, agreeing on the total of 167. Post returns confirm the number: thirty-nine adult males over sixteen; thirty-four males under sixteen; fifty-four adult females over sixteen; and forty females under sixteen.[20]

Among the prisoners, Andrews singled out Shoot-the-Bear and his family of one wife, a teenage son, and a daughter. Major Brotherton at Fort Buford had recently informed Andrews that Shoot-the-Bear had come from the Poplar River Agency in Montana with several other families who were not part of the hostiles that had surrendered with Gall in November 1880. The agent at Poplar River considered the family to belong in his care, and he wanted them back. Brotherton had received orders that these Lakotas were not to be sent down to Fort Yates with Gall's hostiles but were to be kept at Buford until further orders were received. However, Shoot-the-Bear had claimed that he did not belong at the Poplar River Agency, which was home to the Yanktonais Sioux, as he was a member of Gall's band of Hunkpapas, and he had insisted on going to Fort Yates with Sitting Bull's band, presuming that he would be allowed to rejoin Gall's camp. But being with Sitting Bull, he was treated as one of his followers and now found himself at Randall. Andrews immediately had Shoot-the-Bear and his family put back on the *Sherman* to be returned to Fort Yates, "an order which he was only too glad to obey," the post commander remarked.[21]

As for Sitting Bull, he made it known that he did not like having his camp right next to the fort. The Hunkpapas had arrived in the evening, and this campsite was no doubt intended as a temporary one, for as soon as the handover was completed, they received instructions to move their camp to open ground, about half a mile to the west of the fort. Moving to that site, the women soon had the camp erected. It was traditional in style, being a circle of about thirty tipis, all with their entrances facing east. As chief, Sitting Bull's tipi would have been opposite the entrance to the camp, which was a gap on the eastern edge of the circle. All visitors were expected to use this entrance. To do otherwise would not have pleased the Lakotas, as in the old days when they roamed free, anyone entering their camp by any other way was regarded as an enemy. In Sitting Bull's tipi, besides himself, were his two wives, his newborn daughter, his young daughters Her-Lodge-in-Sight and Stands Holy, his teenage son Stood-by-Him, his younger son Crowfoot, and the three-year-old-twins On-the-Hill and Left Him. His teenage daughters, Many Horses and Seen-While-Walking, would either have been in the same tipi or would have been in an adjacent tipi with his mother, his sister Good Feather, his stepsons Blue Turtle and Little Soldier, and his mother-in-law Lost Woman.[22] Nearby were the tipis of Four Horns and One Bull. Sitting Bull's band was made up of twenty-six families, including the families of his relatives—his uncle Four Horns, his adopted son One Bull, and his cousin Bone Tomahawk, the son of Four Horns. One of the families, The Deaf Woman and her two young children, was without a man at its head. There were also six men and one woman on their own.

Outside the camp would have been a few small dome-shaped sweat lodges where the men went to purify themselves before religious or ceremonial occasions or to have a thoughtful and relaxing "sweat" as they called it. The whole camp looked as it would have appeared in the old days out on the plains. However, two ingredients essential to any Indian camp—horses and dogs—were missing. As soon as the camp had been established, the post surgeon, William H. Faulkner, came to check on the health of the Hunkpapas. He treated two of the children, amputating a partially severed finger of one and treating another who had been scalded with hot coffee. Otherwise, the Hunkpapas were in good health.[23]

Guarding these people was the regiment stationed at Fort Randall, the Twenty-fifth Infantry, one of the four African American regiments of the United States Army. The fort served as the regiment's headquarters, housing the band and Companies B, F, G, and

I, a total of 19 commissioned officers, and 216 soldiers of other ranks. The other companies were split between Forts Hale and Meade, also in Dakota Territory. Although these so-called buffalo soldiers, which was the name the Indians had given them, possibly because their complexion and hair reminded them of the buffalo, had not previously served on the Northern Great Plains, the Hunkpapas at Fort Randall would have been aware of their reputation as brave men. Sitting Bull had had contact with one African American before, namely the interpreter Isaiah Dorman, who had married a Sioux woman and was known among them by the name of Teat. Now Sitting Bull and his people were confronted by a fort full of them, but, apart from one instance, the Hunkpapas got on well with their buffalo-soldier guards.[24]

Their treatment as prisoners of war was turning out not to be as bad as they had feared. Andrews was able to report two days after their arrival that Sitting Bull "represents himself as well pleased with his present surroundings, that he is at peace with all the world and intends to remain so, with the exception of the Crows, Assiniboines, and Piegans [Blackfeet], with whom he was not able to make peace before leaving that part of the country. But two questions trouble his mind at this time viz.—why he was sent here and how long he is to stay?"[25]

As prisoners of war, the Lakotas were constantly watched over. From a large guard tent, pitched a short distance from the Indian camp, sentries patrolled the perimeter of the compound day and night. However, the Hunkpapas were allowed to come and go as they pleased within the immediate vicinity of the fort, and they were allowed inside the fort itself. The entire band had to be present at the 9:30 morning roll call, where, sitting in front of their tipis, they were counted by both the old and new duty officer of the day. On the last day of each month, Colonel Andrews took the roll call himself. The event became one of the highlights of their day; the Hunkpapas painted their faces and dressed up for the occasion. The women paid particular attention to their children's appearance, insuring that the younger members of the band were well turned out. Anyone who was ill was allowed to remain inside the tipi, and the medical officer would visit them later.[26]

Daily life in camp was much the same as it always had been. At dawn, they would arise, and the men would leave the tipi while the women dressed and attended to their toilette. Sitting Bull and One Bull would stand outside the chief's tipi and raise their right arms to the sun, singing a prayer of thanksgiving to Wakan Tanka—the Great Spirit. They then returned to their tipis for their first meal. Food was available throughout the day. There were no set meal times, everyone ate as and when they pleased. Meat was the main ingredient, either roasted or boiled. Their rations of beef, pork or bacon, flour, shelled corn, hard bread, beans, coffee, sugar, salt, soap, and tobacco were the same as the soldiers' and were drawn for them from the post commissary. The soldiers also brought over a daily issue of freshly slaughtered beef, which they cut up and distributed to each family. The Hunkpapas could visit the post trader's store, if they wished, to supplement these official rations. The Hunkpapas always offered food to visitors, and it was considered bad manners to refuse. Any food left over could be taken away to be eaten later, but the visitors were expected to return the bowl. Not to do so was again bad manners. For once in their lives, the Hunkpapas had no need to worry about a shortage of food, although they might well have longed for some buffalo or deer meat.[27]

Life for the women and children had not changed dramatically from what they had always been used to. The women's duties remained the same—preparing food, collecting firewood, and performing other household tasks. They still met in groups to gossip while making clothes and decorating items with beadwork. For the young single women, there were a noticeable lack of suitors in such a small, tight-knit camp, but mothers and other female relatives still watched over them. The children entertained themselves. The girls played with dolls and miniature tipis. There were too few boys to organize their old team war games, but they played scaled down versions of traditional ball and hoop games.[28] In quieter moments, the boys sat and listened respectfully to the men talking of their hunting and war exploits. Did they realize that they themselves would not participate in such events when they grew up?

For the men, it was different. Their role as providers and protectors had been suspended. For the most part, all they could do was laze around, smoking and talking of past glories. The relaxation of gambling, associated with games such as the moccasin game, was still possible. This popular game could be played by either two teams or by two pairs of players, and the aim was to guess which hand held the stick. Singing and drumming accompanied the game, and players and onlookers gambled, often quite heavily, on the outcome. It could become quite exciting and noisy as the onlookers shouted encouragement and advice to players.[29]

Feasts and dances were permitted and lightened the boredom of being a prisoner. The dances were usually men only or women only, with the opposite sex present as singers and drummers. Although participants would have been few, it is possible that the Night Dance was held. This formal dance was one in which the young men and women, for once, were allowed to dance together. To get started, girls selected male partners, and each couple danced in a line around the fire, participants holding their partners by their belts as they danced with knees bent in a slow rocking movement in time to the rhythm of the drumming. All dances were accompanied by feasting and went on long into the night.[30] At such times, for a few hours, the prisoners could forget their confinement and make-believe that they were out on the open plains again.

Sitting Bull was allowed to run his camp without interference from the soldiers, and he governed it in the traditional way. In his tipi, he met with the other chiefs and headmen to administer the camp, aided, as of old, by appointed *akicitas* who acted as policemen in carrying out the wishes of the leaders. In the past, this council would have organized communal buffalo hunts, ceremonials, and tribal war parties. Apart from the ceremonials, these events were things of the past, but camp order still had to be maintained.[31] Lieutenant George P. Ahern, Twenty-fifth Infantry, who was stationed at Fort Randall in 1882, later observed: "The camp, like all Indian camps, was well administered by the Chief. Never was there any disturbance. The children were well behaved and apparently never needed disciplinary measures. This was due largely to the love of the children for their parents, and the profound respect paid the older members and leaders of the tribe."[32]

For the soldiers at Fort Randall, the presence of Sitting Bull's band did not alter the routine of their lives. Reveille was at 4:55 A.M., breakfast at 5:30 A.M., sick parade at 6:00 A.M., and fatigue call at 6:30 A.M. At 7:55 A.M. was guard mount. To the accompaniment of the regimental band, the old guard, which had been on duty for the previous twenty-four hours, was replaced by the new guard. The sergeant major inspected both guards, and when he was satisfied with their turnout, they marched to the parade ground, where the officer of the day drilled them before releasing the old guard and sending the new to their various assignments. Those soldiers not on guard duty were given fatigues, which usually consisted of manual work such as cutting wood, repairing buildings, or cleaning. In late 1881 and early 1882, soldiers at Fort Randall were building a new warehouse for the post store. Some soldiers were engaged in duties away from the fort. They were required, for example, to supervise distribution of rations at the nearby Yankton Indian Agency, to assist settlers in the surrounding countryside, and to inspect the telegraph line from the fort to Springfield. The latter was a continuous task.

For troops stationed in the fort, the midday meal began at 12:20 P.M. and lasted forty minutes, then back to work until the evening meal. Five minutes before sundown, the whole garrison paraded in full dress uniform for inspection. Tattoo was at 8:50 P.M., and Taps at 9:30 P.M. Company drills were held four times a week, with battalion drills held twice a week. Target practice occurred several times a week, and many looked upon this activity more as sport than training. There must have been consternation in the Hunkpapa camp when they heard target practice gunfire for the first time. The officers maintained drills and target practice until the winter weather set in, when aiming and distance practices took precedence.[33]

In off-duty hours, the ordinary soldier had little to do. They spent most of their time in visiting and talking, often in the post-trader's store, or gambling. Drinking alcohol was another pastime, although it would appear that the post trader at Fort Randall was forbidden, by official order, from selling alcoholic drinks. Nevertheless there were places outside of the fort, or in nearby Yankton, where liquor could be obtained. For the serious-minded, a library and a reading room offered an assortment of books and magazines. This library and a separate assembly room were attached to either side of the post chapel, which the soldiers had built themselves out of local chalk rock in 1875. When not playing in the settlements and towns in the territory, the regimental band, which had a reputation as one

48 of the best in the United States Army, no doubt gave musical eve-

nings for personnel at the fort, officers and their families getting the best seats, of course. Impromptu singing was common, both during the day at work and in the barracks in the evening. There were some families at the fort, and occasionally dances may have been held, but with a noticeable scarcity of female partners. On Sundays, a church service took place in the chapel.[34]

For the ordinary soldier, there was no fraternizing with Sitting Bull's band. Officers and their wives, together or on their own, were frequent camp visitors, however, and many friendships were established. The wives often brought over extra food to show their appreciation for items of beadwork, such as moccasins and pouches, made for them. Both the Hunkpapas and the whites were surprised at how friendly the others each were.[35]

Once Sitting Bull had settled into his new environment, he determined that it was time for him to meet the president. Accompanied by Allison, who had been retained by the military as the chief's interpreter, he went to see Colonel Andrews, asking him to send a letter to Washington to inform the authorities that he wished to visit them. On 26 September, Andrews sent off the following letter:

At the request of Sitting Bull, I have the honor to state he very much desires to visit Washington D.C. taking with him Gall and other representative men to the number of ten or twelve; failing in this he desires a visit from some one especially commissioned by the President, and failing in this he desires to be informed "over the President['s] own signature" just what it is proposed to do with him and his people, and when.

He says he has acquired a great respect for the missionaries of the Episcopal Church and desires that one of them shall accompany him to Washington. Also that they shall teach his people.

He expresses himself as entirely done with war, and only wishes to know the will of the President that he may obey it.

He also says he is satisfied that the United States is strong and that nothing remains for his people to do, but to go to work as other Indians have done and "raise their living out of the ground."

While professing his entire submission to the United States authorities, and since he has been at this post, he and his people

49

have acted upon this principle, he at the same time expresses the opinion that his people should be taken care of, as he sees other Indians are, and supplied with wagons, plows, white man's clothing, horses, oxen, cows, bulls etc., etc. and that he as a representative man should be furnished with a wagon and a pair of horses.

The present mood of himself and people *with him* is such as to indicate, that, they will submit without trouble to almost any thing reasonable, but under the influence of "hope deferred" its attendant uncertainty and the approaching cold weather, it is possible this mood may change.

All seem to be impressed with the idea that they are now in friendly hands and that their good is considered.

I would therefore venture the opinion that such action as is intended in their case should be speedily taken.[36]

This letter clearly indicates Sitting Bull's attitude now that his circumstances had changed. He was prepared to accept the situation and to lead his people along this new path. At the same time, he made it plain what he expected the government to do for him and his people now that they had given up their old way of life. His request for a wagon and a pair of horses for himself shows that he expected special consideration as the chief of his band. His reception at Bismarck and Fort Yates, the interest and respect civilians and soldiers had shown him since his surrender, all convinced him that he was still an important man. But a special visit to see the president was completely out of the question; it would inflate the chief's ego and signal to the Lakotas that he was still a man of importance and influence. The military definitely did not want to convey this message to him and his old followers. In Lieutenant General Philip Sheridan's opinion, Sitting Bull "is not a chief and never was, and his influence—if he has any—arises more from the notoriety that has been given him than from any talent for leadership that he has ever displayed."[37] The military's attitude was thus ambiguous. On the one hand, they considered Sitting Bull powerless and without any following other than his own small band, but on the other hand, they thought it advisable to keep him away from the rest of the Lakotas.

If the military did not think much of Sitting Bull, most of the general public did, either admiring him or hating him. He always made good newspaper copy. His fame had spread across the United States and Canada and was now extending to foreign countries. All kinds of people were interested in Chief Sitting Bull, and many came to see him or wrote to him during the time he was at Fort Randall.

FORT RANDALL,
SEPTEMBER–NOVEMBER 1881

The presence of Sitting Bull at Fort Randall drew an influx of visitors. While the families of the officers at the fort regularly came to the Hunkpapa camp, the first outsider to visit Sitting Bull was White Swan from the Yankton Agency across the Missouri River. He came a day or two after the chief's arrival, in what, no doubt, could be classed a courtesy call. The Yanktons, or Nakotas, were part of the Seven Council Fires of the Sioux. Although the Yanktons were more sedentary, rather than nomadic like the Lakotas, they were still of the same people. Colonel George L. Andrews had been in charge of Sitting Bull for only five days. He was not sure how the chief was reacting to his confinement, and the colonel worried that the local Indians could have an unsettling effect. However, as a special concession, he allowed White Swan to see Sitting Bull, something Andrews may have soon regretted, for White Swan went back to the agency and told the Yanktons they could visit the Hunkpapas.[1]

On Friday, 23 September, eight Yanktons arrived from across the river, but they were not visitors. The Hunkpapas no doubt watched with interest as this group went straight to the post headquarters. Escorted by Indian policemen Sergeant Poor Bull and Private Fat were three young men whom Yankton agent W. D. E. Andrus wanted confined in the guardhouse for five days. Accompanying them were three friends who wished to "share their *prison joys*" (emphasis in original), the agent said. The reason for the disciplinary measure was not recorded, but Andrews agreed to keep the prisoners for the specified time. He locked the young men in the guardroom, where they had no contact

Sitting Bull's surrender at Fort Buford, Harper's Weekly.
State Historical Society of North Dakota, B1036

Gall. David F. Barry photograph, South Dakota State Historical Society

(opposite) Crow King. David F. Barry photograph, South Dakota State Historical Society

The Merchants Hotel in Bismarck, Dakota Territory.
State Historical Society of North Dakota, C0791

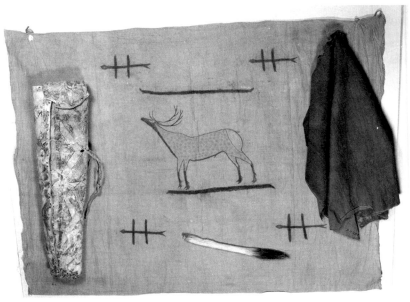

Sitting Bull's Medicine Bag, including a banner that may have been flown from
the steamer Sherman. *USDI, Indian Arts and Crafts Board, Sioux Indian Museum,*
Rapid City, South Dakota

Fort Yates, circa 1889. South Dakota State Historical Society

Pictograph of Sitting Bull counting coup on a white man.
Smithsonian Institution, Three Pictographic Autobiographies
of Sitting Bull *(1938)*

(opposite) Running Antelope. David F. Barry photograph,
South Dakota State Historical Society

Major James McLaughlin.
State Historical Society of North Dakota, A1356

(opposite) Orlando Goff's portrait of Sitting Bull.
Orlando Scott Goff/Library of Congress

Colonel George Lippitt Andrews. United States Army Military History Institute, Carlisle Barracks, Pennsylvania

Fort Randall, circa 1874. South Dakota State Historical Society

The Twenty-fifth Infantry at Fort Randall.
South Dakota State Historical Society

Troops from Fort Randall issuing supplies to Sitting Bull's band.
Bailey, Dix and Mead photograph, South Dakota State Historical Society

with the Hunkpapas. Five days later, on the twenty-eighth, Poor Bull and Fat returned to collect the men.[2]

In a letter, the Yankton agent next informed the colonel that the Indians at the agency had collected a wagon-load of dried corn for the Hunkpapas. The agent was under the impression, conveyed by White Swan, that the colonel had requested extra food for his charges. The Yanktons had collected the food and wanted to bring it across the river. The Yankton chief, Strike-the-Ree, hoped to present the corn personally and also meet with Sitting Bull. Accompanying him would be Medicine Cow, Old Joint, Walking Elk, Running Bull, Grabbing Bear, and the agency interpreter, Charles Picotte. Agent Andrus told Andrews that the Indian delegation would be a good influence on Sitting Bull because the Yanktons were committed to the new way of life. Andrews replied on the thirtieth that he had already told the Indians that he did not need supplies for the Hunkpapas and that he had enough corn at the fort to last several months. If, in the future, he should need extra food for his prisoners, Andrews would contact the agent directly. As to a visit by Strike-the-Ree and the other headmen, Andrews bluntly stated that he much preferred they stay at home. The colonel would, however, allow a brief visit with Sitting Bull, providing the Yanktons called on him first and came dressed as white men. If they appeared in their traditional dress, wearing feathers and with painted faces, Andrews "would march them directly back to the river banks and send them home."[3]

The Yanktons apparently complied with Andrews's conditions, and one of the delegation, Walking Elk, wrote to the colonel on 3 December about the event:

Dear Sir,
    We have talked with Sitting Bull and this is what he said as I heard it and wrote it down:
    From the days of my ancestors the Nation of the Seven Council Fires of Aborigines, who understand each others language have been accustomed to trade with the White People and to be on good terms with them. And after I grew up I was always dealing with the traders and on good terms with them.
    Then there came the treaty making men, and the men with

White Man's ways, and many of my brethren sold their lands to the Grand Father and said they would settle down and be civilized. And they sent word to me to come down to them. I said, Friends wait a little. There are a great many buffalo up here yet. I want to eat meat a while yet. By and by when you get fixed up and able to make a good living at civilized ways I will come down to you, and then I will have my people learn how to make a living that way. So I said, and stayed out in the wilderness and hunted buffalo.

Then the soldiers came and hunted my tracks and as soon as they got in sight of me shot at me, and after they had done that my boys turned upon them. So they chased me for a number of years. And now they put all the blame of this thing upon me. But, friends, I know very well that all the blame does not lie with me. The beginning of the evil was with some of my nation who lived nearer the Whites.

And so I said I would leave that business and come down to where my friends were being civilized, and I sent that word all around, and told my people to lay by their weapons, but they did not want to hear me. So I said—Well the Grand Father has been calling to me to come for a good many years, let us go and see what he wants us for. For me I will go down and get what he calls me for. And so I sent word to my friends who were being civilized at Standing Rock, and Cheyenne River, and Pine Ridge, and Rosebud, and Lower Brule, and Crow Creek, and Yankton Agency, and told them to help me to civilized life.

So I came down. And I saw a Missionary and he told me that the Grand Father had laid down the gun, and that there would be no more hostility, and he said the Grand Father told him to tell me that, and also to tell me to lay down my gun. And so I said I would do it, and I told him to tell the Grand Father, and I told him in what country I wished to settle down to civilized ways. And so I am thinking now how we can get settled down.

I want to settle down to farming with my nation. I know that it is only by the help of the Grand Father and so I want him to help them that they may live. And so I want the Grand Father to give them some of his things. I want him to give a span of horses to each family, and a yoke of oxen, and a couple of plows, and a cow to each. And I want him to give them such things as they will need to live on for a number of years. And I want the Grand Father to give us a location for ourselves where we can have these things.

Then I want to be good friends with the Whites the same as all the treaty Indians. Then I want my people to dress up like White people and live like they do. If I did not want to I would not have come down.

Then I want to make all these arrangements for my people, and in order to do this I want to go and see the Grand Father. I want to go soon this winter, so my people will be ready to settle down and go to work in the spring. I have given up everything my nation had to the Grand Father, so I want to go and see him.

Then my friends, now I have settled down to be civilized, I want my children taught. I want schools and teachers the same [as] you have. That is what I understand the Grand Father wanted me to come in for. So I want my children to have those advantages.

Then I did not come in with one tribe alone. There were some with me from all the Agencies, Standing Rock, Cheyenne River, Red Cloud, Spotted Tail, Lower Brule, Crow Creek, and Yankton, and it is with them all that I want the Grand Father to make the same provisions. That is all.

Now I heard his talk and I think he speaks good words. So I hope you will hear what he says and help him. The Grand Father and the Missionaries want all the 13 tribes of Sioux to be civilized, and now Sitting Bull is the last one to come in and now he says he wants to be a White Man and I hope you and the missionaries will help him.

And now you wanted me to take down Sitting Bulls words and I have, and now I want you to have them printed and sent all round. And I have got Mr. Williamson to translate them as you suggested so it would be correct.

Your Friend
Walking Elk

Witnessed by Running Bull[4]

Sitting Bull did not say anything new in this talk. He still considered himself to be the injured party in his conflicts with the whites. On the whole, he was correct. He had attacked the forts because the soldiers were invading his hunting grounds. Stealing horses from the military was an accepted practice among the Lakotas and was not, strictly speaking, an act of aggression. In this respect, they treated the soldiers no differently from their Indian neighbors. As Sitting Bull often said, all he ever wanted was to be left alone. Unfortunately for the Lakotas, they stood in the way of the opening of the West. While he never openly admitted defeat, Sitting Bull had surrendered and had now to endure the peace. He was wise enough to understand that the Lakotas would have to accept the white man's ways, and the chief was prepared to see that his people got the best deal possible. He himself would not necessarily accept this new order, however. Sitting Bull would always remain a traditional Lakota.

On Monday, 10 October, an unexpected commotion occurred in the Hunkpapa camp. Crazy Dog had appeared as if from nowhere, and his wife Pretty Camp rejoiced in his arrival at Fort Randall.[5] In the confusion and speed with which Sitting Bull's people had been pushed onto the *Sherman,* some families had become separated because husband or wife was away visiting relatives in the main hostile camp. No one had been able to understand them as they pleaded with authorities to wait until their spouses could join them. With such a large camp of ex-hostiles so close to the Standing Rock Agency, the military had wanted to get the chief away as quickly as possible. Crazy Dog had been one of those away, unaware of the imminent removal of Sitting Bull's band. Other Hunkpapas had also been left behind, but Crazy Dog decided to do something about it. Six days after the *Sherman* departed, he had begun a twenty-four-day walk to Fort Randall.

The details of this epic journey were not recorded, but Crazy Dog likely followed the course of the Missouri River, avoiding the white settlements, although he may have found some isolated white settlers from whom he could ask for food.[6] Plants such as the wild turnip, small game, and fish would have been available to him, but with no gun or bow and arrows, which would have been taken from him at Fort Buford, and with only a knife, hunting would have been difficult. If he crossed the Missouri at Fort Yates, he could have traveled through the Sioux reservation past the Cheyenne River Agency, where his fellow Lakotas would have helped him with food. Even so, he faced a walk of about three-hundred miles across what was now white man's land—quite a task for a forty-nine-year-old man.

The night of his arrival, the Hunkpapas likely celebrated the return of one of their number. All would have contributed food from their rations, and no one would have been more generous than Sitting Bull. As chief of the camp, he was expected to provide, and he never let his followers down. On the twelfth, Colonel Andrews telegraphed both his superiors in the Department of Dakota and Colonel William Passmore Carlin, Fourth Infantry, the commanding officer at Fort Yates, informing them of the arrival of this lone Indian.[7] On the seventeenth, Major Breck wrote back to instruct him that Crazy Dog was to "be received and treated as one of the prisoners of Sitting Bull's band."[8]

The next excitement to liven up the Hunkpapa's life of confinement occurred a little over a week later. Captain Paul Boyton, who was on a journey down the Yellowstone and Missouri rivers to the mouth of the latter where it joined the Mississippi, and newspaperman James Creelman arrived at the fort. Boyton was an adventurer who traveled the rivers of the world. He did not use a canoe or boat. Instead, he floated along in a rubber suit he had designed, propelling himself with a two-bladed paddle. For this trip, he had tied a line around his waist and towed behind him a small canvas boat, about four feet long, with the name *Baby Mine* painted on the side. It contained all the necessities for his journey. Traveling with him in a canoe was Creelman, a correspondent for the *New York Herald,* who was reporting Boyton's journey for his newspaper.[9]

The Hunkpapas no doubt inundated Boyton and Creelman with questions about who they were and what they were doing. The officers escorted the men back to the fort, where they were given quarters for the night. The following day, Creelman sought out Sitting Bull for an interview, which was recorded in his book *On the Great Highway*:

Following Sitting Bull to his tepee, I crawled after him through the covered hole which served as a door. We were joined by Allison, the famous white army scout, who acted as interpreter, and by a number of Indians, who entered at the request of the old chief. We seated ourselves on the ground around a heap of burning twigs, Sitting Bull sitting at the head of the circle. He threw aside his blanket, under which he wore a fringed shirt of deerskin. The two wives of the household shook hands with us, giggled, and paraded several half-nude and very dirty children, the heirs of the family.

There was silence in the tepee. Sitting Bull laid his tomahawk and knife on the ground, and began to fill his long pipe with tobacco and killikinick, the dried scrapings of willow bark. No one spoke. The chief looked at the fire, and took no notice of us until he had puffed at his pipe for a few moments. Then the pipe was passed around, and as each man smoked, Sitting Bull watched his face closely. When the ceremony was ended, the old leader gazed at the pink and violet flames flickering among the broken fagots, and pursed his lips. The wrinkles on his forehead grew deeper, and a look of shrewdness came into his dark face. . . . The chief put his thumbs together, as though he were comparing them—an odd trick that I have noticed in other Sioux politicians—and began.

"I have lived a long time, and I have seen a great deal, and I have always had a reason for everything I have done," he said, in a deep, low voice—still staring thoughtfully into the fire. The listening Indians nodded their heads. "Every act of my life has had an object in view, and no man can say that I have neglected facts or failed to think."

He took a long pull at his pipe, and as the smoke glided from his lips he watched it musingly.

"I am one of the last chiefs of the independent Sioux nation," he said, "and the place I hold among my people was held by my ancestors before me. If I had no place in the world, I would not be here, and the fact of my existence entitles me to exercise any influence I possess. I am satisfied that I was brought into this life for a purpose; otherwise why am I here?". . .

"This land belongs to us, for the Great Spirit gave it to us when he put us here. We were free to come and go, and to live in our own way. But white men, who belong to another land, have come upon us, and are forcing us to live according to their ideas.

That is an injustice; we have never dreamed of making white men live as we live.

"White men like to dig in the ground for their food. My people prefer to hunt the buffalo as their fathers did. White men like to stay in one place. My people want to move their tepees here and there to the different hunting grounds. The life of white men is slavery. They are prisoners in towns or farms. The life my people want is a life of freedom. I have seen nothing that a white man has, houses or railways or clothing or food, that is as good as the right to move in the open country, and live in our own fashion. Why has our blood been shed by your soldiers?"

Sitting Bull drew a square on the ground with his thumb nail. The Indians craned their necks to see what he was doing.

"There!" he said. "Your soldiers made a mark like that in our country, and said that we must live there. They fed us well, and sent their doctors to heal our sick. They said that we should live without having to work. But they told us that we must go only so far in this direction, and only so far in that direction. They gave us meat, but they took away our liberty. The white men had many things that we wanted, but we could see that they did not have the one thing we like best,—freedom. I would rather live in a tepee and go without meat when game is scarce than give up my privileges as a free Indian, even though I could have all that white men have. We marched across the lines of our reservation, and the soldiers followed us. They attacked our village, and we killed them all. What would you do if your home was attacked? You would stand up like a brave man and defend it. That is our story. I have spoken."

The old chief filled his pipe and passed it around. Then we crawled out into the sunlight again. As I was about to leave, Sitting Bull approached me.

"Have you a dollar?" he asked.

"I have."

"I would like to have it."

When the silver coin was produced the chief thrust it into the bosom of his shirt.

"Have you another dollar?"

"Certainly."

"I would like to have that, too."

I gave him a second coin, which also disappeared in his shirt.

"Tobacco?"

A bag of fragrant birdseye followed the money.

"Ugh!" said the old man.[10]

Sitting Bull thus closed their meeting, and on 20 October, Creelman and Boyton went back to the Missouri River and continued their journey downstream. A crowd of whites and Lakotas gathered on the riverbank to watch the two men set off, with Creelman in his canoe and Boyton propelling himself along with his double-bladed paddle. Standing on the bank as the pair moved off into the distance, Sitting Bull might have mused that some white people were very strange indeed.[11]

On 23 October, Sitting Bull was in the post store when a white man he had not seen before approached him. The newcomer was Rudolf Cronau, correspondent and artist for a leading German magazine, *Leipzig Gartenlaube*. Because of Cronau's steel-rimmed pince-nez spectacles, the Lakotas had given him the name of *Ista-masa*, which meant Iron Eyes, and Sitting Bull apparently knew of his arrival. Approaching the chief, the journalist greeted him with *"How cola Tatanka-yotanka,"* which translated as "Hello, friend Sitting Bull." Although initially startled, the chief returned the greeting, *"How cola Ista-masa."* No doubt Sitting Bull was surprised to hear Lakota spoken with a German accent. As it was nearly lunchtime and Cronau had already agreed to dine with Regimental Quartermaster Henry P. Ritzius, Twenty-fifth Infantry, who had been born in Prussia and with whom he was staying, he made arrangements to visit the chief that afternoon.[12]

Arriving in the camp after lunch, Cronau went to Sitting Bull's tipi, where they had "a most pleasant talk," with Allison interpreting as usual. At this meeting, the chief agreed to have his portrait painted, which Cronau did two days later on the twenty-fifth. The painting showed the chief wearing a war bonnet with ermine-tail pendants, which Sitting Bull would probably not have possessed while he was a prisoner, but he approved of Cronau's work and signed the painting for him.[13]

60 Cronau stayed at Fort Randall the longest of any of Sitting Bull's

visitors, but during this time, another group arrived who were to be of great help to the chief. As he sat for his portrait, these visitors, whom Sitting Bull had invited, arrived at the fort. They were Thomas H. Tibbles, his Omaha wife Sussette ("Bright Eyes"), Alice Fletcher, an Omaha man called Wajapa, and Buffalo Chip and his wife Gaha, who were Poncas. Fletcher, a budding ethnologist, intended to study the manners and customs of the Indians, particularly the role of women in Indian life. She was forty-three years old and single. Tibbles was forty-one years old and a white man well known to the Omahas and Poncas, although he was less familiar to the Sioux. He had a fiery nature and embraced a cause with passion, particularly that of the Poncas. Tibbles claimed to be responsible for Judge Elmer S. Dundy's historic 1879 decision in *Standing Bear* v. *Crook* that the Indian was a person. From 1879, Tibbles had spent the winters in the eastern United States lecturing on behalf of the Indians. At one of these lectures, he first met Fletcher, who asked if she could accompany him on his next visit to the Indians. Tibbles was at first reluctant to take her out West, but she eventually convinced him that, although an eastern lady, she was fully aware of the hardships she would have to endure to visit the Indians. He finally agreed to let Fletcher join him and his wife on their summer trip to see their friends among the Omahas and Poncas and to visit the Sioux. By nature, Tibbles was egotistical and short-tempered, and Fletcher was a determined woman. The two did not always get along, but they never had a serious falling-out during their travels together.[14]

Sitting Bull, who knew of Tibbles's reputation as a defender of Indian rights, called upon him to help the Hunkpapas. Knowing that Tibbles intended to visit the Yanktons, the chief secretly arranged for a messenger to ride up to the Rosebud Agency, where Tibbles and his party were staying, and invite them to visit.[15] This unexpected invitation was too good to miss. The journey to Fort Randall was difficult, dangerous, and took a week, during two days of which they were snowbound. Arriving at the fort, the party set up their camp at the northwest edge and then all went over to report to Colonel Andrews. Fletcher had letters from government officials authorizing recipients to extend her all courtesy and to help with her study of Indian life. While they were talking to Andrews, the colonel's wife came into his office and, after being introduced, invited Alice Fletcher to stay with them, although Tibbles may not have been happy with this touch of favoritism.[16]

The next day, the twenty-sixth, Tibbles went to Andrews to complete the formalities that would enable the party to visit the Hunkpapa camp. The rest of the day was spent in looking around the fort. At dusk, hearing the band playing, the group, minus Fletcher, went to watch the dress parade. Later, as they were returning to their tent, Sitting Bull and three other Hunkpapas approached them. The translation of their ensuing conversation took some time. Sitting Bull spoke to Buffalo Chip, who translated the Lakota into Ponca for Sussette Tibbles to interpret into English for Tibbles, and then the complicated and time-consuming process began in reverse when Tibbles spoke. The chief said that he was worried about a problem, but he could not discuss it in front of a woman and he wanted his official interpreter, Allison, sent away and someone else to translate for him. That night, Tibbles arranged for permission to visit Sitting Bull and found an Indian who could speak English—Charles Picotte, interpreter at the Yankton Agency and stepson of Sitting Bull's friend Matilda Galpin.

The following morning, Tibbles and Picotte went over to the Hunkpapa camp. Sitting Bull first wanted to know how long Tibbles could talk to him. Whatever that time was pleased the chief, and he agreed to talk that day of his main trouble, which proved to be his interpreter. The United States government had sent Allison to Canada to encourage him to surrender, Sitting Bull said. Allison became the chief's official interpreter, and he assumed total authority over Sitting Bull's band. If the Indians did not do what Allison wanted, he told them that he would have them all sent to the Indian Territory, an effective threat. The Hunkpapas knew all about Indian Territory, where a great many Indians died from homesickness and from diseases such as malaria.

During his first week as interpreter, Allison took a young girl as a wife with no courtship or payment to her family, as was Lakota tradition. Sitting Bull regretfully told the girl's father to let his daughter go with the interpreter. Later, Allison demanded the wife of one of the headmen. A reluctant Sitting Bull again told the husband that, for the good of the people, he would have to let his wife go. What emotions this poor husband and wife had to endure can be imagined, but there was nothing they could do. Allison did other bad things, but Tibbles considered them "too vile to record." Sitting Bull was sure that the officers at the post did not know what was going on in his camp.[17]

Knowing of Sitting Bull's discontent, Allison must have had an inkling that the arrival of Tibbles would give him problems. He had previously warned the chief that a man was coming with his women, and that he should not listen to him. The women were good for nothing, and the man had stolen a Winnebago woman. He was not to be trusted, and he could not do anything for him. Sitting Bull ignored Allison's warning and, in speaking to Tibbles, he had complained to the right man. Tibbles was an activist, and he took up Sitting Bull's plight with his usual enthusiasm.[18]

Upon leaving the chief, Tibbles went to Captain Charles Bentzoni, Twenty-fifth Infantry, the acting commanding officer at Randall—Colonel Andrews and his wife having left that day for Chicago—and reported all that the chief had told him. The captain was angry. He had been led to believe that Allison was a friend to the Hunkpapas. He was disgusted with the man and promised to look into the matter immediately. Word quickly spread around the officers at the post, and they found Allison's conduct equally appalling. Life was getting difficult for the interpreter. Alice Fletcher, when she heard, went to Captain H. Baxter Quimby, Twenty-fifth Infantry, and also complained. Quimby agreed to help Sitting Bull, and Allison was not present at a subsequent meeting between the chief, Tibbles, and Fletcher. Bentzoni contacted the Department of Dakota headquarters to report Allison's behavior and asked what action he should take. On 3 November, he received orders from Major Breck to send Allison to Fort Buford, where he was to report for duty. The whole affair was an embarrassment for the military, and they hushed the matter up.[19]

After Tibbles had reported to Bentzoni, he and his party returned to the Hunkpapa camp at about 12:30 P.M. At the chief's tipi, Sitting Bull greeted them with "much state," Fletcher reported. Another twelve or thirteen men soon joined the group. The pipe was lit and passed around. Sitting Bull spoke "in a low tone, with much deliberation," saying that his people were now divided into two factions—those who were prepared to change, and those who were not. The older men were too old to change their ways, the chief said, but the younger men would have to change for the sake of the women and children. Because there was no game to hunt, he wanted cattle, chickens, and hogs. He wanted his people to learn how to farm, but they had not been given the tools to do so. He wanted an agent that was wise and good. He wanted to go to Washington to see the president and had written a letter to that effect. His people were in need of warm clothing, and he wanted extra rations, because the children got hungry. It would be hard for him to change, but the children could learn the new ways. The occasion had turned out to be a solemn one, the only interruption being when one of the chief's wives came in to add sticks to the fire. She knelt on the floor beside Fletcher and, leaning on her elbows, studied the white woman's features. Fletcher later recalled that the wife had a "handsome face," with "sparkling eyes," and wore shining brass bangles on her arms.[20]

The twenty-eighth of October was rainy, and everyone stayed indoors. Winter was approaching, and after roll call on the following day, the Hunkpapas moved their camp from the open land west of the post to the wooded area to the north, where it could be protected among the trees. Although Fletcher was leaving that day, difficulties crossing the Missouri delayed her departure for several hours. The removal of the camp was a good opportunity to learn more about the role of women in Indian society, and Fletcher went over to watch. First, the family goods were packed into parcels, and then the women, with the help of their daughters, started to take down the tipis. Sitting Bull's tipi came down first, then the others followed. The women first removed the wooden pegs at the base of the tipi that held the cover taut over the framework of poles. Then they removed two poles that supported the smoke flaps. Then they took out the wooden pegs above the entrance, freeing the cover to be rolled up by two women working in opposite directions until they met at the back. Then they took out the back pole and laid it on the ground so that the cover could be untied and folded into a tight parcel. Finally, they took the tipi poles down.

In better times, the women would have fastened the poles to waiting horses to form a travois, in which the tipi cover and the family baggage could be placed for the move, but the Hunkpapas now had neither horses nor dogs, which had been used for the same purpose in pre-horse days. The women most likely dragged the loaded tipi poles over to the new campsite, a distance of over three hundred yards. At the new location, the same procedure was undertaken in reverse. It took about fifteen minutes to erect or dismantle a tipi. While all this activity was going on, the men sat in a line in the center of the old camp circle, smoking their pipes and chatting. When the women had finally finished, the men got up and strolled across to the new campsite—the older men going last. Sitting Bull, wearing his incongruous goggles, was the last person to move.[21]

Once they had all settled down, Fletcher, accompanied by Picotte, went over to say goodbye to her new friend. She recorded her talk in her field diary:

Told Sitting Bull I had been thinking of what he told me and of how I could help him. The head officer was away but I had spoken to one of the other officers & he will come & see Sitting Bull & Charlie shall interpret. Sitting B. can trust the officer & must tell him all his troubles—tell him everything. I was going far away to the East and would tell his friends there the good words he had spoken. Sitting Bull said—what he had said was still in his heart he had no other words. The nephew of Allison has struck one of his young men. It was very hard to endure, but he remembered what I had said & have the young man keep quiet, but it was very hard. I told him to tell the officer everything. He said they had not enough to eat often they went to bed hungry. I made same reply. He said it was [tiresome?] staying here—his heart was tired. He did not understand it how long would it be. I told him to keep up a good heart not to feel tired it was very hard & I was sorry but it would be a long time very likely. He wanted to see the [President] & would like to go with young Spotted Tail. When could he go. I didn't know—a long time. The children had no blankets. I said I would try & help them but it would take a long time.

   Could he send the little children to the mission. He wanted them to learn the better way. Could he send them. I said I would write to the Col. . . . He pulled off his ring—said I have nothing to give, keep this to remember me. It was very touching.[22]

65

With anxious faces, the women and children gathered about Sitting Bull as he said goodbye and invited Fletcher to return. He assured her that he meant what he said about leading his people to a better life. Before leaving, Fletcher gave the chief two dollars to spend on his children. Some of the women brought their young babies over to Fletcher so that she could shake their hands. She wrote in her field diary, "God help me to help them."[23]

Before her visit to the Sioux was over, Fletcher went to say goodbye to her friend Captain Quimby. She told him of the talk she had just had with Sitting Bull and what he was asking for. Quimby promised to relay the information to Colonel Andrews when he returned. She gave the captain another two dollars to give to Sitting Bull for his family.[24]

During the time that Tibbles and Fletcher were at Randall, Rudolf Cronau was also still there. The three must have had some contact, but none of them mentioned any meetings. Cronau remained at Fort Randall for several weeks, becoming good friends with Sitting Bull. They tried to teach each other their languages, but with little success. Sitting Bull would have had little opportunity to speak German; nevertheless, he tried. Cronau did successfully teach the chief how to draw horses. Sitting Bull's later pictographs showed a more realistic portrayal of that animal than most Indian paintings of the period. Before coming to Fort Randall, Cronau had spent some time at Fort Yates and painted a series of portraits there. Colonel Andrews now invited Cronau to put on an exhibition of these portraits at Fort Randall. On the first day, the exhibition was open to the officers and their wives. The Hunkpapas, who viewed the paintings on the second day, were enthralled by what they saw, recognizing friends and family from Standing Rock Agency.[25]

When it came time for Cronau to leave the fort in mid-November, he went to the Hunkpapa camp to say his farewells. He found Sitting Bull in his tipi with some of his headmen. Cronau gave the chief a photograph of himself that Sitting Bull had asked for as a memento of his friend. The chief's last words, as recorded by Cronau, were in the style of a dime novel, but the sentiments were true: "*Ista-masa*, come back, and you will find us always as your good friends. May the waters carry you safely, and may *Waka-tanka*, the Great Spirit, preserve you from all dangers!"[26]

The first two months of captivity at Fort Randall were over. Sitting Bull had had productive visits with Fletcher, Tibbles, and Cronau. Allison's removal must have made him realize that there were white people who would help him and his band. The Hunkpapa leader had begun to share his people's suffering more openly with these visitors, and he may well have had hope that his other requests would soon be attended to.

FORT RANDALL,
NOVEMBER–DECEMBER 1881

Rudolf Cronau left Fort Randall in mid-November 1881, but he was still there when an important visitor arrived to see Sitting Bull—the Vicar Apostolic of Dakota Territory, Bishop Martin Marty. At the end of May 1877, when he was still Abbot Marty, the bishop had visited Sitting Bull in Canada in an unsuccessful attempt to encourage the hostiles to surrender.[1] Marty had become bishop on 1 February 1880 and undertook a tour of his diocese in the fall of 1881, visiting Indian agencies and white settlements. Because he was based at nearby Yankton, one of the first places he visited was Sitting Bull's camp at Fort Randall. Apart from a brief mention in the *Yankton Daily Press and Dakotaian*, few details of this encounter are known. The newspaper reported that the bishop found the chief satisfied with treatment at the fort and ready to take up farming and teach his people this new way of life. Religion would naturally have come into the two men's conversation, but the article does not indicate whether Sitting Bull wanted his people to be Christianized or not. Although the chief himself had no intention of converting, he might have agreed to the possibility in order to get the bishop on his side. Sitting Bull needed all the influential friends he could get.[2]

On 11 November, Colonel Andrews, the post commander, received a letter from Bishop Marty:

> My dear Sir,
>   Knowing you now as well as I do, I have no doubt that you do not wish to exterminate but wish to civilize the Indian. An important step towards this end can never be taken to better advantage than now with the Indians under your care. They are kept in one

place, at leisure in body & mind & in every way ready to learn and improve. If I could place a missionary there, who could see them once or twice a day, they could achieve that full religious instruction & training, which they need to make their material advancement next spring rapid, successful and permanent. The priest, whom I would like to send after receipt of your consent, would board with Mrs. Pratt, who is a Catholic & act in accordance with your orders. He knows the D[akota] language & can do his work without troubling any body. You will have the kindness to present to Mrs. Andrews the homage of my sincerest regard and gratitude.

Please direct your answer to
Your humble servant
Bp. M. Marty[3]

That same day, Andrews wrote back that he could not sanction Marty's request and that it was a matter for "higher authority."[4] Andrews appears not to have been enthusiastic over this request; his letter was brief and to the point. A missionary teaching these most traditional of Lakotas a new religion might have unsettling effects. For the moment, the Indians were causing no trouble, and Andrews intended to keep it that way.

At the same time Marty was making his request, Episcopal Bishop William H. Hare was writing to Secretary of War Robert T. Lincoln. Sitting Bull had asked to have some of his band's children placed in the care of the Indian boarding schools that had been established near Fort Randall, and Hare wanted permission to comply. Alice Fletcher, who was now at the Santee Agency, also wrote to Lincoln, duplicating Hare's request. Lincoln referred the proposal to the secretary of the interior, and that is where the matter rested,[5] as the Roman Catholics and Episcopalians vied to have Sitting Bull and his band adopt their particular forms of Christianity. Both bishops sought to introduce the Indians to civilization through education and Christianization, two intertwined objectives, but both men wanted to convert Sitting Bull first in the hope that all the other Lakotas would follow. As it turned out, Sitting Bull became quite adept at playing one off against the other.

The Episcopalians had the advantage, however, for they often provided material help. Evidence suggests that Bishop Hare had visited the Hunkpapa camp even before Bishop Marty arrived, and on 5 November, Hare sent a box of clothing over to Fort Randall, asking Colonel Andrews to distribute the garments among the Lakota families. He had noticed "the naked condition of many of the children in Sitting Bull's camp," he explained. Hare may have been worrying unduly because young boys often played around camp naked, particularly in warm weather, as they had when they roamed the Plains in better times. No Lakota parent would allow a child to suffer unduly from the cold, but an Episcopal bishop may have found the nudity troubling on many levels. In any case, the Lakotas would have welcomed the extra clothing as winter approached.[6]

On 28 November, another lone Hunkpapa arrived at Fort Randall, probably by boat. His name was Many-Old-Men, and he was crippled from a dislocation of his left knee. The new arrival had a twenty-day pass from Cheyenne River agent Leonard Love to see his sick wife, who was with Sitting Bull's people. Like Crazy Dog and his wife, Many-Old-Men and his wife had become separated in the rush to get Sitting Bull's band aboard the *Sherman* at Fort Yates. Andrews wrote to his superior, Major Breck, asking what to do about the visitor as he obviously belonged with Sitting Bull's band. Andrews also informed Breck that he knew of three more Lakotas who were attempting to come to Fort Randall. As there were several unattached adults in the Hunkpapa camp, these three may have been missing partners. However, the post returns for Fort Randall, which included a count of the Indian prisoners of war, showed no increase in adults for December 1881 or January 1882. Either Andrews refused any passes, or the missing Hunkpapas did not turn up. For Andrews, these Lakotas alleging to belong to Sitting Bull's band were problematical. The colonel had an official list of his prisoners that had been made out when the Hunkpapas arrived at Fort Randall. He had not received the original list made at Fort Yates at the time of their removal, however. Andrews considered this second list essential in making proper identification of his charges and accordingly requested a copy.[7]

On 9 December, Andrews experienced another problem that made him wish for an accurate list of his prisoners. Following the roll call, the officer of the day reported one Hunkpapa missing. On the following day, the count produced the same result. On the eleventh, all prisoners were reported present, but on the following day, one was again missing. The Hunkpapas insisted all along that nobody was absent from their camp. Andrews apparently never identified the missing prisoner, although he suspected it was one of the young women.[8]

Winter had descended on Dakota Territory, where it could be unpredictable and extreme. During a mild spell, it was possible to go about without a blanket or an overcoat, but the following day could bring a fierce blizzard. Winds whipped fallen snow into an ice dust that penetrated everything, turning clothing into frozen suits of armor. No human or animal could face into such a blizzard, which was capable of freezing eyelids shut. Even when there was no snow, the icy wind itself was dangerous. In the old days, the Lakotas knew to pitch their camp in sheltered areas where the weather could be tolerated. The previous winter of 1880-1881 had been a particularly bad one, with snow falling to a depth of eleven feet during a nineday blizzard in February. As they hunkered down for their first winter as prisoners of war at Fort Randall, the Hunkpapas could take some solace in the fact that they were not totally isolated, and food should be available no matter the weather.[9]

On 12 December, one of the first deaths occurred in the Hunkpapa camp when Sitting Bull's aunt, the wife of Four Horns, died. Because uncles were on the same kinship level as fathers, Sitting Bull would have felt the loss keenly. The usual funeral rites would have been observed, although whether her body was placed in a tree or scaffold somewhere in the surrounding countryside, as was traditional, or was interred in the post cemetery is not known.[10]

Sometime before 12 December, Sitting Bull received a visit from Captain Gaines Larson, commander of I Company, Twenty-fifth Infantry, and the Reverend John P. Williamson, who was the Presbyterian missionary at Yankton Agency. The pair produced a scrapbook for Sitting Bull to look at. Opening it to the first page, Sitting Bull saw a drawing of himself as a young boy of fourteen counting coup on a warrior who was preparing to fire an arrow at him. As he turned the pages, which contained more of his war exploits, Sitting Bull realized that these drawings were copies of a series of pictographs that he had made about ten years earlier for his adopted brother, Jumping Bull, who had still had them when he visited the chief that summer at Fort Yates. The images had been made on the back of muster-roll blanks of the Thirty-first Infantry, which measured ten by eight inches, and had been pasted onto the pages of the book. In all, there were fifty-five drawings—fifteen portraying the exploits of Jumping Bull and forty covering Sitting Bull's activities in the period from 1846 to 1869, his most active years as a warrior. The Sitting Bull pictographs showed him receiving twelve honors in fights with Indians (mostly Crows), sixteen in fights with white men, and twelve in horse raids against both Indians and whites. Given his earlier care not to mention these exploits to reporters, Sitting Bull must have been somewhat alarmed to see this evidence of his warlike past spread out before him. Why was he being shown this scrapbook? Although he got on well with these people, they were, after all, white men, and experience had taught him that you could not always trust a white man.[11]

Williamson, who was fluent in Lakota, told Sitting Bull that the book had been sent from the Army Medical Museum in Washington so that the chief could give a true and accurate interpretation of the drawings in his own words. Whatever misgivings he may have had, Sitting Bull agreed, possibly because Williamson's command of Lakota was so superior to that of previous interpreters, allowing the chief to converse with him man to man. Williamson and Larson sat and listened as Sitting Bull gave an account of his war exploits, although the chief would not go into much detail concerning the war honors he had earned in combat with white men. Both Williamson and Lawson were convinced that "any narration he gave of the several events was colored by the circumstances of his present situation."[12] Williamson suggested that a fuller account of these events could be obtained once Sitting Bull had settled down to his new way of life, but in the years to come no one followed through on this idea. For his services, the military paid Williamson twenty-five or thirty dollars, plus five dollars traveling expenses.[13]

Also at this time, the post commander received a request from Captain William P. Clark, Second Cavalry, for details on Sitting Bull's movements after the Custer battle. Lieutenant General Philip H. Sheridan, commander of the Military Division of the Missouri and a Civil War hero, had commissioned Clark to produce a work on Indian sign language and the habits and customs of the Plains Indians.

With an interpreter of Williamson's competence on hand, Colonel Andrews took the opportunity to provide Clark with the chief's story. For his part, Sitting Bull was much more open on this subject than the previous one, and he gave details of his journeys after the battle. Williamson was then able to make a map, drawn under the watchful eye of the chief.[14]

Williamson transcribed Sitting Bull's words in a letter to Colonel Andrews dated 12 December 1881:

After the Custer Fight (June 25th 1876) the whole camp moved southwest to the mountains, thence south along the foot hills east of the headwaters of the Big Horn for some distance. After some time they turned north-east to the headwaters of the Rosebud, then down the Rosebud, then turning more east they crossed the Powder River and other streams, following into the Yellowstone, and made a circuit crossing the headwaters of the Grand River, going as far south as the Slim Buttes.

As fall drew on they turned north towards the head of Powder River. A short distance before they reached Powder River the camp divided. One party, which he thinks was the smaller one under Crazy Horse went west to the Big Horn River. Soon after the other party under Sitting Bull, moved north, going down the east side of the Powder river they crossed the Yellowstone a short distance below the mouth of the Powder river. The Yellowstone was not yet frozen when they crossed, but it was cold. Going on north, after spending some time hunting buffalos, they reached the Missouri river soon after it was frozen over, crossed over at the mouth of Milk river, and camped on that stream, but did not go up it far. While on Milk river a considerable party under "Long Dog" left his camp and went on north to Canada. Sitting Bull soon returned with the body of Indians to the head of Powder river, where they spent most of the winter. Towards spring Crazy Horse, with the rest of the Indians who had gone to the Big Horn in the fall, went east to the Agencies, and he saw Crazy Horse as he passed. Soon after this Sitting Bull's camp again divided. One party under "Red Horse" and "Four Horns" going direct to the British Possessions. This party crossed the Missouri river near Old Fort Peck. Sitting Bull followed a little later with his party, crossing the Yellowstone at the old place, and the Missouri river a little below the mouth of the Muscleshell [*sic*].

The ice in the Missouri broke up two days after they crossed. They went directly on to Canada, and met the other bodies who had preceded them, at Wood Mountain, according to previous agreement when the grass was green.

Soon after their arrival in Canada, they had a big council of the Indian tribes. After this his people hunted buffalo along the line, sometimes coming south as far as the Missouri river. During one of these expeditions his people came in contact with American troops, who had marched up from the Yellowstone. In this brush four of his men and one woman were killed. This must have been in 1879.[15]

Once again, Sitting Bull was unwilling to discuss confrontations with the troops sent out after him. He made no mention of skirmishes with the military at Cedar Creek or Ash Creek, relating only an attack while his followers were hunting south of the Canadian border. Sitting Bull's reticence is a pity for history, but his caution in dealing with his former enemies is understandable. In 1884, on his first tour East with showman Alvaren Allen, the chief's speeches of peace would be "translated," unbeknownst to him, as lurid and sensational accounts of the Custer fight. In reality, however, the chief was modest and circumspect. George P. Ahern, who arrived at Fort Randall in September 1882 with the rank of second lieutenant and became Sitting Bull's friend, recalled that the chief would often speak of hunting and traveling but would say nothing of his battles with white or Indian enemies.[16]

When Christmas celebrations began at Fort Randall in 1881, it was just another day for the Hunkpapas. Both Bishop Marty and the Reverend Williamson would have told them all about the birth of Jesus. Some of the Indians, out of curiosity, may have wandered over to the fort to see what the soldiers were doing. Services at the chapel and the singing of carols to the accompaniment of the regimental band may have marked the holiday. The Hunkpapas might have marveled at how the families in the fort decorated their quarters. Perhaps some of the officers and their wives came over to Sitting

Bull's camp in the afternoon with gifts for the children. Who knows? No record survives of this special day at Fort Randall.

Two days later, on the twenty-seventh, any goodwill between the Hunkpapas and their guards was put to the test. Towards noon, a distraught young Hunkpapa woman returned to the camp—she had been raped. Sitting Bull and his headmen no doubt held a council to decide what action to take. In the old days, justice for this offence, rare within a tribe, would have been immediate. The woman's husband or, if she was unmarried, her father and brothers could have killed the rapist, or the policing *akicita* society, who carried out the chiefs' orders, could have killed the man's horses and destroyed his tipi. If he were lucky, the rapist may have been allowed to make reparations through his family to the woman's immediate relatives in the form of horses and material goods. The rapist's family would have been deeply shamed, and the man responsible may have had to leave the camp. Times were different now. Sitting Bull, as leader of the camp, accompanied by some of the *akicitas*, probably took the woman and her male relatives over to the fort to see Colonel Andrews, the only person able to administer punishment.[17]

Andrews was shocked. The woman, Spirit Cane, had gone to the wooded area north of the fort to collect firewood; there she was assaulted by three soldiers, two of whom raped her. Andrews immediately assembled the whole command on the parade ground. Sitting Bull and others from the camp probably watched as Andrews escorted the woman along the ranks of his soldiers, from whom she confidently picked out her attackers—recruits Edward Mack and Robert Lincoln. A third recruit named Lumney, also of I Company, confirmed his part in the attack, deserting less than two hours after Mack, the ringleader, was put in the guardhouse. Witnesses testified that they had seen the three men going in the same direction as the woman. Andrews no doubt assured Sitting Bull that the soldiers would be punished, and the sight of the men placed under guard and escorted to the guardhouse may have given the Hunkpapas some satisfaction. The white man's law was not so drastic as Lakota law, however. In the end, Andrews chose to dismiss the men from the army and thus avoid any publicity, which would have harmed the African American regiment. In addition, Andrews concluded that the case would not get a fair hearing in a civil court. Under frontier justice, Indians had no rights. In addition, the victim would have testified through an interpreter, whose translations were not always reliable. Therefore, the whole affair was hushed up.[18]

In fairness to the troops at Fort Randall, the three accused men were recruits, and they must have joined the regiment with the typical frontier opinions of Indians—views that were not necessarily shared by the veteran troops. The four Buffalo Soldier companies stationed at the fort had good reputations. They were among the best-behaved troops on the frontier, with low rates of alcoholism and desertion, good discipline, and high moral conduct. Their severest critic, General of the Army William Tecumseh Sherman, said of African American soldiers: "They are good troops, they make first-rate sentinels, are faithful to their trust, and are as brave as the occasion calls for."[19]

Such sentiments offered small comfort to the aggrieved Spirit Cane and her family, however, although the offending soldiers had, in effect, been exiled from the community. To avoid future incidents, Captain Charles Bentzoni ordered the Hunkpapas to keep away from the fort except at certain times. The Indians would be allowed to visit the post trader's store between the hours of 3:00 P.M. and 5:00 P.M. on weekdays. During those times, the troops were forbidden to go the store.[20] As the year 1881 ended, the Hunkpapas found that white man's justice sometimes resulted in greater restrictions on the Indians' movements.

FORT RANDALL,
JANUARY-APRIL 1882

The new year may start on 1 January for the white man, but for the Hunkpapas, the new year would not start until the spring. What strange people these whites were to begin a new year in the middle of winter. Yet, in January 1882, the Hunkpapas began a new life, too—they sent their children to school.

For some time, Sitting Bull had realized that the future well-being of his people lay with the young. The young could adapt, and he reasoned that if the children were educated by the white man and learned his language, then they would achieve a form of independence and see to it that the white man did not cheat them. In all his speeches following his surrender, Sitting Bull always mentioned his wish to have the children go to school alongside his other requests—or demands, as some saw them. He had so impressed Alice Fletcher with his acceptance of change that she was keen to help him in any way she could. After leaving Fort Randall at the end of October 1881, she crossed the Missouri River to the Santee Agency, where she stayed with the Reverend Alfred R. Riggs. In conversation with Bishop William Hare, the three had decided upon a joint approach to fulfill Sitting Bull's wishes in regard to the children of his band. To have the children of the leader of the hostile Sioux and his immediate followers under their tutelage would be quite an achievement for the Episcopal church.

Following a series of letters among the War and Interior departments, Bishop Hare, and Miss Fletcher, Colonel Andrews informed Hare that he had received authority to accede to the bishop's wishes to educate some of the children from Sitting Bull's band. Andrews now inquired, how many boys, how many girls, and of what ages could

77

the school accommodate? Many of the parents objected to sending their children away, Andrews said, and convincing them would not be easy. Once they got used to the idea, however, Andrews hoped that some of the parents would change their minds. The fact that Sitting Bull was in favor of the plan and would send his own children would help. Only healthy, intelligent children could go, but parental consent was essential. Andrews had found six boys that met his criteria—a son and two nephews of Sitting Bull, the sons of Looking-Back-Bear, Man-Who-Takes-the-Gun-Away, and Man-Who-Wears-Fur-Coat (Hairy Coat).[1]

On the twenty-eighth of December, Bishop Hare had replied that he could accept three boys and two girls, aged between ten and fourteen. The boys would attend Saint Paul's school at Yankton Indian Agency under the charge of Mr. Henry E. Dawes. The girls would attend Saint Mary's school at the nearby Santee Indian Agency and would be under the charge of Miss Amelia Ives. On arrival, they should all report to Dawes, who would arrange for the girls to be sent to Santee in the bishop's own private conveyance. The bishop requested that Sitting Bull and the other fathers accompany the children and stay for a day's visit. The fathers could then see the school and the dormitory where their children would be staying. Such a visit might put their minds at rest, Hare said, and a good report from Sitting Bull would be helpful.[2]

Andrews responded with disappointment at the low numbers. He was confident that he could enroll more boys, although the numbers of girls would always be small. He needed to know what the future prospects were for an increase in pupils so that he could decide whether to continue his efforts in persuading parents to let more children attend schools. The good news was that Andrews was able to inform Bishop Hare, in a letter dated 30 December, that he had obtained three boys and two girls for the mission schools, namely:

Small [Little] Soldier, 13 years of age, [step]son of Sitting Bull
Charge on the House, 13 years of age, son of Fur [Hairy] Coat
Rock, 11 years of age, son of Looking-Back-Bear
Yellow, 11 years of age, daughter of Man-Who-Takes-the-Gun-Away
Bread, 14 years of age, daughter of Big Leg.[3]

Andrews had explained to the fathers, in detail, what would happen to their children in school and how they would be looked after, and the parents gave "their full and free consent," he told his superiors. The fathers of the children would be allowed to accompany them across the Missouri to the mission school, where they could stay the whole of that first day with them. After the daily roll call on 4 January, and tearful goodbyes from their mothers, these children and three of the fathers—Sitting Bull, Hairy Coat, and Big Leg—proceeded under a small military escort, across the Missouri to the mission school.[4]

At the chalkstone school, *Zitkana duzahan*, or "Swift Bird," as the Yanktons called the bishop, greeted the delegation. Hare had earned the name for the way in which he moved swiftly from camp to camp and agency to agency within his diocese.[5] He introduced the Hunkpapas to the headmaster of the school, Mr. Dawes, and to the teachers and the housemother, who escorted them around the building—the hall, classroom, dining room, and kitchen, all on the first floor. On the second floor and in the attic were the dormitories, all heated by sheet-iron stoves. Bishop Hare himself had determined the operation of the school:

My plan is to make the School so far as possible *self-serving*, i.e., to make the boys take care of themselves and of the house. For this purpose they are divided into three squads and to each squad is assigned for one week one particular department of work. One squad is the Dormitory Squad, whose duty is to make the beds and keep the dormitory and some other rooms in order. Another squad is the Table Squad, whose duty is to set the table and wash the dishes, etc. A third is the Outdoor Squad, whose province it is to bring wood, run errands, go for milk, etc. Each day when the several squads have discharged their respective duties, they all unite and work at levelling and cleaning up the grounds. . . . By ten o'clock all manual work for the morning is over and the boys go into school for two hours. Then dinner and recess till two o'clock, then work again till three, then school till five.[6]

Although the school did not impose the harsh military-style discipline that typified Carlisle and Hampton, the larger Indian boarding schools in the East, the squad system of work may have dismayed the boys. Bishop Hare found that his first pupils, the Yanktons from the agency, took "to work better than I dared expect. Perhaps novelty gives the task a charm."[7] The children were principally at school to learn how to read, write, and speak English—exactly what Sitting Bull wanted and had often asked for. He knew from experience that not being able to speak the white man's language had put him at a disadvantage. The bishop, too, was well aware of the disadvantages of working through interpreters, and he had originally planned to master the Indians' languages, but, like Sitting Bull, he eventually focused on preparing the children for the new life, and apart from church services, Hare relied on an interpreter.[8]

Later the same day, the Hunkpapas returned to Fort Randall, and the officer in charge of their escort reported to Colonel Andrews that the arrangements were "entirely satisfactory" to the fathers.[9] Arriving back at the camp, the men would have been met with a barrage of questions. Sitting Bull's wife, Seen-by-the-Nation, would have been anxious to know how her son Little Soldier had reacted to the school. No doubt, the chief shared the full details of his visit with his wife and, quite possibly, held council to relate the events of the visit. As his people had no previous knowledge of children attending the white man's school, he would have done his best to reassure them that all would be well and that it was in the best interests of the children that they now learn the white man's ways.

With winter in the air, Andrews had immediately turned his attention to getting provisions for the Hunkpapas. When Sitting Bull's band surrendered at Fort Buford, the army had given them blankets to cover their tattered clothes. Some of the Hunkpapas had obtained extra clothing from various post traders, bartering what few possessions they had, and the bishop and other visitors to the camp had given the Hunkpapas some used items. It was obvious that they would need extra clothing, for they were unable to provide for themselves. In September 1881, the interpreter Allison had written to Colonel Andrews with an extensive list of supplies that the Hunkpapas needed:

1500 yds Calico   40 Butchers Knives
120 Flannel Shirts   120 Thread—spools

160 yds, List cloth (probably "Strouding")   40 Needles–papers
170 Deer skins–dressed   40 Combs–hair, coarse
200 Blankets, woolen   40 Combs, hair, fine
40 Camp Kettles   60 Thimbles
30 Frying pans   60 Scarfs, woolen
120 Tin cups   60 Shawls, woolen
60 Gloves or mittens, pairs   200 Sinew, pieces
100 Socks, men's, pairs   40 Axes & Handles
40 Skins–par fleshed   30 Coffee Mills
40 Coffee Pots   40 Bake Ovens
100 Handkerchiefs   40 Buffalo robes–3rd rate for moccasins
80 Bed sacks
40 Scissors pairs   600 feet Rope ½ inch
1000 Yds Dress goods, cotton and wool (for the women)
Canvas for 4 Lodges, or equivalent to 12 A tents

Submitting this list to his superiors, Andrews gave his opinion that some of the quantities were "in excess of the quantity required." For instance, he noted, one thousand yards of dress goods would give the fifty-four women in camp two dresses each. The fifteen hundred yards of calico that topped the list would make an additional three dresses for each woman.[10] Allison may well have inflated quantities so that he could siphon off items for his own private disposal. The Hunkpapas could not have complained, for he was their voice where the government was concerned. Andrews submitted a revised list to the Department of Dakota in October, but by January 1882, two and a half months later, nothing had been received.[11]

The need for adequate clothing had been undeniable, however. Back at the end of October 1881, the acting inspector general of the Department of Dakota, a Major Saunders, had inspected Fort Randall and reported that the Hunkpapa prisoners were suffering from lack of suitable covering for their feet. He suggested then that one hundred pairs of buffalo overshoes in the fort's stores, which were no longer required by the troops, be given to the prisoners so that they could make moccasins out of them. On 3 December, Major Breck had ordered Andrews to release the overshoes to the Hunkpapas. They needed more than moccasins, though, and as leader, Sitting Bull would have been constantly asking that the needs of his people be met, embarrassing Andrews with queries about when the supplies would arrive. On 3 January 1882, Andrews asked Breck for permission to supply a few blankets from his stores to the prisoners who, now in the middle of the Dakota winter, were desperately in need of them. Breck responded that blankets were among the items from the original October list that he assumed had been sent over two months ago. On the thirteenth of January, Breck telegraphed the colonel, asking him if he had received any of the clothing from the October list. Andrews replied on the seventeenth, "Neither clothing nor invoices have been received." On the twenty-first, Andrews again advised Breck that he had not received any clothing or invoices. On the twenty-third, Major General Alfred Terry received a telegram from Robert Williams, assistant adjutant general of the Military Division of the Missouri, advising him that the clothing requisition had been forwarded to the adjutant general on 27 October.[12]

Obviously, an interdepartmental mix-up had occurred somewhere along the line. The problem lay in the War Department's lack of money for purchasing goods and clothing for Indian prisoners of war, whom they were holding at the request of the Interior Department. Letters had gone back and forth between these two departments concerning the problem, but basically, neither could afford to keep the prisoners. The War Department struggled to maintain supplies for their troops and had little surplus. The Bureau of Indian Affairs, a division of the Department of the Interior, likewise had no surplus funds. The War Department had handed over 2,829 Sioux hostiles to the bureau in July 1881, and these earlier surrenders had cost the bureau an estimated $195,000 for goods and supplies. Transportation added extra costs, leaving the bureau short of funds, if indeed they had any left. In the end, the War Department found the money to keep the Fort Randall prisoners by creating a deficiency. When the Bureau of Indian Affairs submitted to Congress their estimate of required funding for the next fiscal year, they agreed to request sufficient funds to reimburse the War Department for monies that it was now spending in the Indians' behalf; for the present, the War Department would take fiscal responsibility for supplying the Hunkpapas at Fort Randall.[13]

The secretary of war, in a letter dated 17 February, told the secretary of the interior, that, considering the "urgencies of the case this Department deems it proper to provide the necessary clothing and other articles for these Indians, and to continue to feed them until they can be taken charge of by the Indian Office. Instructions will therefore, at once be sent to the military storekeeper at Philadelphia to purchase such articles of needed clothing as are not already on hand, and to prepare the packages and send them by fast freight with all possible dispatch."[14] Sometime towards the end of February, then, the much-needed supplies eventually arrived at Fort Randall.

Finally the women could make new clothing for their families. The forty buffalo robes originally requested were vital in replacing their worn-out moccasins. There was, however, a problem—they had no sinew with which to sew the moccasins. On 18 March, the depot quartermaster at Saint Paul informed Andrews that no sinew could be found and asked if thread would be suitable. The colonel replied that a strong thread suitable for moccasin-making would do and requested that a third of the amount requisitioned should be of this quality and the balance in a thread suitable for making garments. When the thread arrived, it proved to be totally unsuitable and was not even given out to the Hunkpapas. Later in the year, Andrews would again ask the depot quartermaster for two hundred pieces of sinew, but he was told that none were available and again was asked if thread would do. No record exists of how the problem was ultimately resolved, but Lakota ingenuity came up with some alternative or they would have been walking around on bare feet.[15]

In January 1882, smallpox had broken out in several cities and towns in the United States, and as a precaution, the military authorized the vaccination of both soldiers and Indians in Dakota Territory. On 23 January, Fort Randall's post surgeon, William H. Faulkner, was sent to Fort Keogh to carry out vaccinations at military posts and Indian agencies in that vicinity. He was back at Fort Randall on 25 February, when he vaccinated the troops and the Hunkpapa prisoners. The older Hunkpapas were well aware of the deadliness of the white man's diseases. The Lakotas had suffered epidemics of measles, chickenpox, and smallpox in 1837-1838 and 1844-1845.[16] They knew the effects such diseases had had on the Arikaras, Mandans, and Hidatsas, almost destroying their populations completely. A council would have been held in which Sitting Bull and his headmen could persuade the people to let the white doctor vaccinate them. The younger elements in camp may have opposed the idea, but in the end, the council's decision prevailed. On the day appointed, the Hunkpapas went over to the post hospital where Faulkner and the hospital matron were waiting for them. A *Saint Paul and Minneapolis Pioneer Press* reporter was on hand, recording "some lively experiences as the young bucks especially have a holy horror of the surgeon's knife and the pale faces' smallpox medicine. One likely young buck about sixteen years old, a son of Sitting Bull, managed to get away from the doctor twice before he was finally corralled and held up by his polygamous sire while the virus was applied, as it were, on the fly."[17] Given his age, the son concerned would have been Blue Turtle, who was a deaf mute and may have found the whole process inexplicable.

The newspaper also reported on Dr. Faulkner's proposal to move Sitting Bull and his band to Yankton Agency, where the Hunkpapas would be under the control of officers from the Interior Department who could instruct them in the "usages and arts of civilization."[18] The *Yankton Daily Press and Dakotaian* reported that the Yankton Indians were prepared to give up some of their land for this purpose, but they expected to be paid for it. Whether this proposal called for a permanent settlement or just an alternative to Fort Randall is not clear, and official records make no mention of it. It is doubtful if Sitting Bull knew anything of the idea. He wanted his people to return to their friends and relatives at Standing Rock and certainly would have opposed the plan. According to Faulkner, some of officers at Fort Randall favored a move to Whetstone Agency, twenty-four miles above the fort, where the chief would be sufficiently removed from large groups of Sioux to cause no trouble. They totally disregarded his stated acceptance of a new lifestyle and recognition of the futility of fighting the white man. The officers argued that in the case of an outbreak there were sufficient troops at Forts Bennett, Sully, Hale, and Meade to suppress it—more than enough soldiers to contain Sitting Bull's forty or so men capable of bearing arms, if they had any to bear.[19]

On the morning of 17 March, the officer of the day reported to Colonel Andrews that one of the prisoners was missing. An interpreter and four of the Hunkpapas were immediately sent out to look but were unable to find him.[20] The missing man was Scared Bear, an old man whose face was drawn to one side "by paralysis." He had been ill, and authorities feared that he had now become insane. Andrews on 21 March informed the agents at Standing Rock, Lower Brulé, and Rosebud that if Scared Bear turned up at their agencies he was to be taken into custody and held until arrangements could be made for his return to Fort Randall.[21] On 4 April, Andrews received a reply from Agent W. H. Parkhurst at Lower Brulé that Scared Bear had been seen in the Lakota camp at the mouth of White River, about seventy-five miles from Fort Randall. Parkhurst doubted that, given the distances, Scared Bear could be caught before moving on. Agent James McLaughlin at Standing Rock replied on 7 April that "diligent" inquiries had failed to locate Scared Bear at his agency.[22] Nothing would be heard of Scared Bear again until July, when McLaughlin would belatedly informed Andrews that the old man had made it to Standing Rock, on foot, and had been there for some time.[23]

About the middle of April, as the Hunkpapas prepared to move out of their winter camp, they received a visit from another photographer. This person has sometimes been identified as Stanley J. Morrow from Yankton or as William R. Cross of Niobrara, Nebraska. He arrived with his wagon, carrying his photographic equipment, portable darkroom, and studio. The Hunkpapas were familiar with photographers. Their first photography session had occurred in Canada, where an unknown photographer took a photograph of them at Fort Walsh in 1878.[24] The sight of a white man setting up his darkroom in either a portable tent or the back of his specially designed wagon was not entirely new to them. Some were skeptical of this *wakan*, or "magic," that captured images of their camp and the Hunkpapas themselves, but Sitting Bull did not seem to mind.

They watched the photographer set up his large, tripod-mounted, stereo-plate camera, snap the shot, and then quickly run into his darkroom to develop the glass plate. If it was Morrow, he was using the wet-plate method. In the darkroom, he covered the glass plate with wet collodion, and placed it in a light-tight holder with a sliding front, which he put on the back of the camera. When his subject was ready, he slid the cover off the holder, making an exposure by removing the lens cap for one to several seconds, depending on the light conditions. He then replaced the cover over the glass plate and dashed into the darkroom for developing. The whole process probably took no longer than ten minutes, for if the plate dried out it was useless. His sitters, however, would have to have been patient, for only a few photographs could be taken at one time. The Hunkpapas must have found the process tedious, but no doubt an audience surrounded the photographer, and it added interest to long days. They would not necessarily have seen the finished results, though, as the prints made from the negatives, on albumen paper, would not be printed until the photographer returned to his main studio.[25]

No doubt the photographer had to pay his Hunkpapa sitters a dollar or two for the privilege of taking their pictures, particularly Sitting Bull who never missed an opportunity to make some money. It was one of the white man's ways that he had quickly adapted to, but he often gave much of the money away, which was not the white man's way. The camera fascinated Sitting Bull, and the photographer explained how it worked, even allowing the chief to take a photograph of one of the Hunkpapa men wrapped in a blanket.[26]

The photographer stayed at Fort Randall for several days, taking photographs both before and after the Hunkpapas moved to their summer camp on the flat land nearer the fort. He photographed Sitting Bull and his family at least four times on two separate occasions and took some pictures of the troops in Fort Randall itself. He also set up his portable studio, where he took portraits of Sitting Bull, One Bull, and Steps, the Shoshoni-Bannock who had lived with the Nez Percés and joined the Hunkpapas in Canada. A photographic firm based at Fort Randall and run by Joshua Bradford Bailey, Dr. George P. Dix, and John L. Mead bought the resulting stereographs and marketed and sold them individually or as a packet of twenty-four.[27] These famous photographs document Hunkpapa camp life at Fort Randall and some of the visitors who came to see Sitting Bull.

Other small social events broke the pattern of everyday life for Sitting Bull, who periodically visited his friend, the Reverend John Williamson. Two armed soldiers waited outside the reverend's house while Sitting Bull went inside. The Williamson children found the soldiers and their guns more impressive than the famous Sioux chief who was talking to their father. Williamson was a man of some influence to whom Sitting Bull could talk without the need of an interpreter. To Williamson, the chief no doubt voiced his concerns over the future of his people and repeated his willingness to accept a new way of life. Sitting Bull wanted to join his followers at Standing Rock, and the reverend agreed that he should be allowed to go there. It was what they both considered best for the future of the Hunkpapas. Williamson was aware that Sitting Bull himself did not deem it possible for the old people to change fully, but he had hopes for the next generation. If the two men discussed religion, the conversation would have been low key, and neither Williamson nor Episcopal Bishop William H. Hare put any pressure on Sitting Bull to change his ways and become a Christian. Sitting Bull and Williamson may have visited the children who had been sent to the school at the agency. The youngsters had settled into their new environment and their teachers considered them good pupils. It would have been good news for Sitting Bull to take back to anxious parents in his camp.[28]

After the Hunkpapas' move to their summer camp, a Yankton Indian named Edward Santee arrived with his wife for a visit on 29 April. His was not a spur-of-the-moment arrival. He had obtained permission to visit the Hunkpapas and arrived at headquarters with a letter that Reverend Williamson had written for him, explaining that Santee's brother-in-law belonged to Sitting Bull's band and the couple wished to visit him. Colonel Andrews was away at a court of enquiry in Saint Paul, but the acting commanding officer, Captain Charles Bentzoni, accepted Williamson's recommendation to permit the visit and issued a pass for the couple to stay in the Hunkpapa camp until guard mount of the day following their arrival. At the end of the visit, they reported back to the adjutant's office to return their pass. Visiting Fort Randall's prisoners was no easy matter, whether you were an Indian or a white man, and all visitors had to follow similar protocol to see the prisoners of war.[29]

FORT RANDALL,
MAY-AUGUST 1882

During the month of May, one male and one female baby were born in the Hunkpapa camp, although, sadly, both infants died within a week of their birth. These were the first children to die in the Hunkpapa camp since their arrival at Randall. Another girl under sixteen years of age and a male over sixteen also died.[1] This sudden increase in births and deaths among the prisoners appears to have prompted Colonel Andrews to order the post surgeon to make "professional visits" to the Hunkpapa camp after daily roll call, accompanied by the old and new officer of the day. The post adjutant, First Lieutenant David B. Wilson, Twenty-fifth Infantry, referred to it as the prisoners' version of the army's sick call. Any Hunkpapas who were unwell were examined and treated accordingly. If necessary, further treatment during the day was allowed.[2]

The women in camp took care of childbirth, as they always had in the past, but deaths were different, and the medical officer had to be notified. Lieutenant George P. Ahern recalled that on one occasion he and the post doctor heard "a loud wailing" coming from one of the tipis. On entering, they found a man laid out for burial. The doctor examined the body only to find that the man was unconscious, not dead, and the wails and tears turned to smiles and cries of joy. The Lakotas were used to this turn of events. In the old days, a body laid in a tipi for a day and a night in case the person revived.[3]

Outside of births, deaths, and illness, the Hunkpapas had little to keep them busy in their summer camp. Tribal war-parties, hunting, and ceremonial events that had filled the men's days before captivity were not possible. Making matters worse, visitors kept them informed of the activities of Lakotas on the Great Sioux Reservation. In June, the Brulés near Rosebud Agency held an unusually large Sun Dance, with thirty to forty men participating in the self-torture part of the event. In the old days, the Sun Dance was the highlight of the Lakota year. Various ceremonies and rehearsals preceded the actual Sun Dance, which lasted four days and culminated with the sun-gazing ritual. Participants who had vowed to sacrifice their own blood underwent self-torture that took several forms according to the participants' wishes.[4]

At the Sun Dance held that summer, not only did a large number of Sioux attend from the different agencies, but over three to four hundred Indians came up from Nebraska, among them at least two hundred Winnebagoes, Poncas, and Omahas. The military received reports that these travelers were well armed and "very saucy and very annoying" to the white settlers they met.[5] Friendly Indians told the settlers that there was potential for an outbreak. In two petitions to Colonel Andrews, the local whites requested that at least two companies of soldiers be put into the field to protect them. As it turned out, the threats were idle talk but did prompt Andrews to send Companies B and G, under command of Captain Bentzoni, to Holt County in Nebraska just in case of trouble.[6] The whole of the Sun Dance festival passed without incident, and the Rosebud agent was able to report, "The Indians never were more peaceable than this summer."[7]

Primarily Brulé and Oglala Lakotas attended this Sun Dance, many of whom had also been part of the coalition of hostile Sioux in 1876, but the Hunkpapas and Sihasapas of Standing Rock were not present. Their agent, Major James McLaughlin, was decidedly against the Sun Dance and would not give permission for any of his Lakotas to attend.[8] In any case, they were busy elsewhere. In the spring of 1882, after an absence of fifteen years, the buffalo had returned to Dakota Territory. This northern herd—the southern herd having been destroyed by the year 1875—contained fifty thousand buffalo that surfaced in the valley of Hiddenwood Creek, about ninety miles from Fort Yates. Major McLaughlin permitted a hunt to be organized, and two thousand Hunkpapas, Sihasapas, and Yanktonais left the agency on 10 June for one of the last great buffalo hunts. The major and his son also participated. Present were many famous leaders of the northern Lakotas—Gall, Crow King, Running Antelope, John Grass, and Rain-in-the-Face—but no Sitting Bull. They killed five thousand buffalo in a traditional summer hunt, complete with feasts and dances.[9]

The news that Lakotas elsewhere were enjoying a buffalo hunt and a Sun Dance, as of old, had an unsettling effect on Sitting Bull and his small band, who were totally isolated and still uncertain of their future. Would they forever be confined at Fort Randall? The young men became restless, some of them threatening to leave if nothing was done, declaring that they would rather die in the attempt to escape than to continue in this state of uncertainty.[10] Colonel Andrews was well aware of this attitude, and in a letter to Major Samuel Breck, assistant adjutant general of the Department of Dakota, he pointed out that his prisoners had been at his fort for ten months without any knowledge of the government's plans for them. "If, as every one knows, a continued state of suspense even when unaccompanied by a feeling of undefined dread of what the future may have in store, is very trying to any human being, how much more so must it be to an Indian situated as the Indians are, reasoning from his own standpoint," he asked the major rhetorically. Although the Hunkpapas had been well behaved, causing no serious problems, "Idleness appeared to be breeding mischief, as quarrels among themselves are becoming more frequent."[11]

In late June, the discontent surfaced dramatically. Two young men made "violent advances" to the belle of the camp, the daughter of White Dog. Her father immediately attacked the two men, putting one of them in the post hospital "with a clean cut in his head exposing the brain."[12] White Dog now feared that if the man died he would suffer the same fate as Crow Dog, who had been arrested and imprisoned for the killing of Spotted Tail.[13] On the following night, White Dog secretly left the camp, taking with him his eldest son, Good Bird. Sitting Bull, on learning that White Dog was missing, "made such dispositions" to ensure that the missing man's family did not join him, reasoning that if they stayed in camp, White Dog would eventually return. Colonel Andrews did not send troops out after the father and son. A heavy rainfall had washed away all tracks, and in any case, Andrews had no trackers or horses with which to follow them. He did not think it wise, given the Hunkapas' state of mind, to send out "any young men from the band" to find White Dog as he had done earlier with Scared Bear. In addition, he worried that, having sent out two companies to appease the settlers in Nebraska, his garrison was now sufficiently reduced that the Hunkpapa young men might think they could attack the fort, take what supplies they needed, and leave if he sent out any more soldiers. Sitting Bull, for his part, undoubtedly knew that such an attack would be futile and worked to contain the young hot heads. Andrews wrote to the agent at Rosebud, where he believed White Dog was heading, asking him to tell the Hunkpapa that the man he had attacked was recovering and no harm would come to White Dog if he returned. He also requested the agent to return White Dog to Randall at the earliest opportunity.[14]

Since their surrender, the dangers of the night had changed for the Hunkpapas. They no longer had to watch for Indian enemies intent on stealing their horses or for white soldiers who suddenly attacked their camp. But the month of June brought other dangers. Just before 4:00 A.M. on the twenty-fourth, the Hunkpapas woke to the noise of strong winds vibrating their tipis and moving the flaps so that smoke from their fires filled the interiors. Torrential rain struck the tipi covers, adding to the din. From each tipi, someone had to go into the storm to push the tipi pegs farther into the ground, while others tried to brace the tipi poles from inside; all to no avail. The whole camp was soon laid flat, and the people had to find what shelter they could in the nearby wooded area, where the wind whipped the branches off the trees and through the air. At the fort, everything moveable blew across the parade ground. Wagons and ambulances flew along at a rate no driver ever envisaged, tumbling end over end until they broke up into a pile of splintered wood. The tumult lasted for an hour, and then the wind suddenly abated.[15]

In the aftermath, the Hunkpapas scoured the area for lodge poles and tipi covers as they put their camp back together. Several families may have had to share tipis until replacements could be made from what material they could salvage or the soldiers could help with. At the fort, fencing, chimneys, ceilings, porches, and the blacksmith's shop had been blown down. The west and north chapel walls were pockmarked with debris driven into the chalkstone. For the next few days, the fort, too, was a hive of industry as the soldiers did their best to repair the damage that nature had done in just over sixty minutes. Fortunately, no fatalities or serious injuries occurred among the Hunkpapas or the soldiers. The wind currents had produced a "tornado, with some of the characteristics of a whirlwind, accompanied for a short time by torrents of blinding rain, and some hail," Andrews reported. It was one of the severest wind storms the colonel had ever seen.[16]

Less than a week later, at the beginning of July, Colonel Andrews had the sad duty of notifying the Hunkpapas that the eleven-year-old daughter of Man-Who-Takes-the-Gun-Away and Yellow Horned Woman had died at Saint Mary's school on the afternoon of 30 June. She had been buried in the cemetery at the Santee Agency the following day.[17] For the parents to send this child off to the unknown school had been hard, and now she was dead and buried in a place that they had never seen, and never would see. She had not died alone, however, and the parents had known that she was ill. At the beginning of May, the superintendent of Saint Mary's, Amelia Ives, had reported to Andrews concerning the illness of one of the girls who came from Sitting Bull's camp.

Her Lakota name was *Hin-zi-win*, but at school she was known as Gertie Bell. When she arrived, the teachers "noticed how round shouldered she was & tried to encourage her to sit up straight," Ives related. Later, they noticed that she often groaned in her sleep and developed a cough that became more pronounced as the weeks went by. She also began to complain of "severe pain in [her] stomach & liver." The agency doctor who examined her found that she had the symptoms of "malarial poisoning" and prescribed iron and quinine. The medicine eased her groaning at night, but Gertie's posture became increasingly worse, and the doctor diagnosed a severe case of curvature of the spine. The doctor also noticed a "dullness" in one of her lungs. Her teachers became even more concerned when they observed that she was refusing to ride in the school wagon as its movement was painful to her. When asked, the little girl said she had fallen while playing in the camp at Fort Randall and that her mother had obtained some medicine for her from the post surgeon. Ives now wrote that she believed the child should go to a hospital, preferably to the new children's hospital in Omaha. She had written this detailed letter to the colonel to ask for his advice about what to do for Gertie.[18]

Andrews replied that his post hospital could treat the child as well as anywhere else. If the young girl wanted to return to her family instead, he added, she should be allowed to do so. Unfortunately, no funds were available for the welfare of the Hunkpapa prisoners, but if Ives would have Gertie sent by boat to Yankton Agency, then the colonel could arrange for a carriage to bring her back to the fort. Ives replied on 19 May that the girl did not wish to leave the school. For the time being, Ives wrote, the staff at the school could look after her and later she could be sent to the hospital at the Yankton Agency. The child had been made comfortable in an adjustable invalid's chair. Ives expressed her hope for a visit from the post surgeon because the doctor at the Santee Agency stated that he was unable to help her any further. She had consulted with Bishop Hare, and they had decided to send Gertie, at the school's expense, to the hospital at Yankton Agency. The woman who was currently looking after Gertie could look after the girl there.[19]

In spite of the care and concern, Gertie Bell died six weeks later.[20] Ives promised to write to Gertie's parents to tell them all about her, but the letter does not survive. The matron's sentiments would have been similar to those she shared with Andrews. "Gertie was a very bright, sweet child & we had all become very much attached to her," Ives told the colonel.[21] Most certainly, the child's death would have raised concerns among parents with children in the schools at the Yankton and Santee agencies. Andrews and Sitting Bull, whose stepson was at the school at Yankton, would have had their hands full assuring parents that the other children were happy and healthy.

As the camp absorbed this loss at the beginning of July, Bishop Martin Marty began one of his tours of his diocese. Leaving Yankton on the fifth, the bishop stopped at Fort Randall to meet with Sitting Bull. A letter he had recently received from trader J. B. Hassett had told him that the chief was disheartened because nothing had been decided about the future of his people and that his young men were becoming increasingly restless and difficult to control.[22] This information may well have prompted the bishop to make a visit to the Hunkpapas a priority on his tour. He arrived at the camp on Sunday the ninth, and talked with Sitting Bull, who expressed his usual wish to be sent back to Standing Rock to start a new way of life. No one, he told the bishop, could determine what plans the government had for his future, and all this uncertainty was putting a strain on his people. Marty was genuinely concerned, so much so that he wrote to Father J. B. A. Brouillet at the Catholic Indian Bureau in Washington, D.C., a few days later. He "could not help feeling the deepest compassion for [Sitting Bull] and his people," the bishop said, asking, "Cannot you do anything at all to obtain mercy & justice?" He suggested that if the authorities were afraid of having the chief so close to his old followers then they should consider Whetstone, the old Spotted Tail Agency, as a suitable alternative. It was only twenty-five miles away from the troops at Fort Randall in case of trouble.[23]

During their visit, Sitting Bull had allowed Marty to baptize three sick women in his tipi. Maria, Anna, and Felicity became the first Catholic converts in Sitting Bull's band of Hunkpapas. The chief, though, had no intention of changing his own religion. He let Marty think differently in order to please him and enlist his aide in his attempts to settle the future of his people. The ploy worked. Bishop Marty left Fort Randall, wrote his letter, and continued his tour. By the beginning of August, he was at Standing Rock Agency, which the Catholics had been allocated in the distribution of Christian missions at the different agencies as part of President Ulysses S. Grant's Peace Policy toward the Indians. The policy divided the Indian agencies among various church groups in the hope that religious oversight would negate the influence of corrupt Indian agents at those sites. In discussions at Standing Rock, Marty and Major McLaughlin decided that the only way to shorten Sitting Bull's captivity and fulfill his wish to be back with his people was to send a petition to Washington. The Hunkpapas and Sihasapas at the agency had already asked for the chief's return, and a petition signed by Sitting Bull would add to the argument.[24]

On 15 August, Hassett took the resulting two-page petition over to Fort Randall, and after it was interpreted for Sitting Bull, the chief duly signed it. It read:

The undersigned respectfully represents that he is an Uncpapa Indian, that his friends & relatives reside at Standing Rock Indian

Agency, that the country, where said Agency is located, has as long as he knows been the home of his people, that whilst he has never signed any treaty with the United States authorities or partaken of any of the benefits of said treaty, he has consequently never violated any of them; that in the spring of 1881 being desirous of changing his mode of life, he voluntarily surrendered to the U.S. authorities in good faith upon the promise that full pardon for past offences would be granted & that he would be located among his people at the Standing Rock Indian Agency; that as a prisoner of war he has quietly & unmurmuringly accepted the situation & remained under the surveillance of the military at Fort Randall notwithstanding the fact that [all] his relations & companions have been transferred to the care and guidance of the civil branch of the government & distributed among the different Agencies to which their respective band or tribe belonged.

In view of those facts your petitioner humbly & respectfully begs, that he & such of his people, as are now held in custody at Fort Randall, be released & turned over to the care & management of the U.S. Indian Agent at Standing Rock, where he pledges himself to remain among his own people the Uncapapas quiet & peaceable conforming himself in every respect to the orders and regulations governing the Indian Service.[25]

Bishop Marty contacted Father Brouillet in Washington regarding the petition and asked for his help. The bishop suggested that the petition should be shown to United States Representative Peter Deuster of Wisconsin, a Roman Catholic, who was aware of the situation and could go to the Indian Office with some influential friends to convey their opinions on the matter. In applying this pressure, Marty had two motivations. He sought to improve the Hunkpapas' situation, but he also aimed to get Sitting Bull back to Standing Rock, where he would be under Catholic influence, and thus "save him from Episcopalian hands."[26] The effort for conversion was a bit late; Hunkpapa children were already being taught in Episcopalian schools, and the chief was having regular visits with his friend John Williamson, the Presbyterian missionary. However, Marty continued to entertain hopes that Sitting Bull would eventually convert to Catholicism.

95

Meanwhile, Alice Fletcher had returned from Washington to the Great Sioux Reservation to study the summer dances, among them the White Buffalo Festival. In late July or early August, Fletcher arrived at Fort Randall eager to learn all she could from the Hunkpapas about the ceremony.[27] Within Lakota society, ownership of a white buffalo hide, whether acquired by hunting or barter, entailed certain obligations and rites that the owner had to undertake; thus, only a rich man could afford to own one. The hide itself had to be specially, and ceremonially, prepared. A young woman, who had to be a virgin, tanned the hide during two days of ceremonies. Each day, she undertook the work dressed in a new set of the finest clothing the hide owner could provide. The secret ceremonies took place within a circle of boughs, and ritual elements included special preparation of the ground, wild goose down placed into holes made in a special black earth, and words that had to be spoken precisely as directed. In addition to the young woman, the only people allowed in the circular enclosure were the hide owner, a holy man in charge of the ceremony, his assistant, the chiefs of the band, a near relative, and the four sons of the hide owner (four sons were necessary to keep the hide). At the end of the actual ceremony, the holy man instructed the owner to be generous to orphans and people who visited his tipi. The hide itself was cut into three strips and distributed among the owner and the chiefs. At the end, the owner made gifts to the poor and to the holy man and his assistant. He then gave his clothes away until he stood naked. Next, he made his way back to his family, where friends soon arrived with new clothes and a new tipi.[28]

Alice Fletcher did not actually see this ceremony, but an old holy man and a few chosen men who understood the ceremony told her the details of it and re-enacted parts for her. Her subsequent description of the White Buffalo Festival, published in 1884, contained much information, but she did not name her instructors. It is probable, however, that the chief she mentioned in her account was Sitting Bull, for such a sharing could not have taken place without his presence.[29] Some problems did arise during the three days of instruction, and Fletcher noted that an atmosphere of dread pervaded the camp because people feared that disaster would follow the revelation of such secrets:

When that point of the description was reached [that] referred to the black earth, the old priest, who was talking, was interrupted by one of the younger men, a person of unusual intelligence and vigor. He rose and with eyes fixed on mine advanced directly toward me and halting regarded me with closest scrutiny. After an awe-inspiring silence he extended his hand in greeting. Then he said "We pray by these things and they are great. We never talk about the white buffalo skin except when we drink water at counsel feasts. You have tried to help us and you are the first and only person to hear of these things." I replied that from my heart I thanked them for what they told me, that the white people knew little of the Indians' religion and only the Indians could explain it. The more they told me the more I could help them.

The chief then told the men who were describing the ceremonial to be very careful not to make a mistake or miss a word lest evil befall them.

As I entered the chief's tent one day, one of the leading men came rapidly toward me, naked and angry. Other Indians followed him into the tent. The priest said, "Evil has come to us!" An Indian repeated angrily, "Yes, evil has come to us of your talking." "My friends, what has happened?" I asked. "A woman was nearly drowned [and] this man"—pointing to the naked person who had followed me into the tent—"hardly saved her." Another man added, "A child nearly choked to death coughing." The men who had talked with me seemed troubled and embarrassed. The chief sat with his head down, drawing figures on the earth with a stick. The other men were very angry. It was a critical moment, but rising and crossing the tent, I extended my hand to the naked man, saying: "Friend, it is *good* fortune, the woman did not drown, you saved her," and turning to the other man I added, "and the child got well." This new aspect of the case being borne out by the facts met with approbation, for the naked man accepted my hand and then resumed his clothing. The others all proffered me their friendship. In view of the supposed bad fortune only two men, who were, however, the most important ones, were willing to talk, and they thought it best to adjourn to some distance from the tent where we might be quite unobserved. They painted themselves for the occasion, with red on their faces and blue stripes on their hair. Their pipe was also freshly painted red.

Before resuming the narrative the two men seated themselves toward the sunrise, lit the pipe, bowed to the earth and passed it, uttering a prayer. They were very serious and anxious that no mistake should occur. They would not draw any diagrams but allowed me to draw some, and corrected my mistakes. . . .

At the close [of the narrative] the younger priest said, "Look at me. I look at you and I shall never forget you. Look at me, you are never to forget me." Then as he paused for my reply, I said, "I am glad you will never forget me for you will remember the face of a friend, and I shall not forget you." Then rising he approached me and with great earnestness fastened his eyes upon me, saying, "Promise me that no harm shall come to me or my people because of what we have told you," and I said "I do not think any harm will come to you because you have talked to me." A second time he asked my promise and I made the same answer. Meanwhile the old priest sat bowed to the earth, and evidently reciting some formula. A third time, with increased earnestness the same assurance was asked and I made the same reply. Then coming still nearer and looking at me with an expression I can never forget, as it showed me how profoundly sacred had been their disclosures, he said: "Promise me by your God, that no harm shall come to me or to my people because I have spoken to you of these sacred things." I answered, "My friend, you ask me to promise you that which only God himself could promise. I will pray my God that no harm shall come to you or to your people because you have talked with me." Then extending my hand, which he took, this strange scene came to a close.[30]

The fact that the Hunkpapas allowed Alice Fletcher to learn the details of this ceremony was a further indication of Sitting Bull's change of attitude. A few years earlier, he would never have permitted it, but he recognized that times had changed for him and his people. Whether he acted out of foresight, realizing that sharing was one way to preserve the old Lakota traditions for future generations, or some other motive is open to debate. In part, Fletcher's interest in the facets of Indian life that touched upon the role of women may have lead the chief to choose her over another confidant. The chief liked Fletcher. She was honest and straightforward, and he trusted her. Her help in ending the dominance of the odious Allison was a point in her favor. She was also genuinely interested in the old ways of the Lakotas and, at the same time, spoke of helping with the future of his people. Perhaps he reasoned that, by letting her learn of the Hunkpapa's secret ceremony, they would cement their friendship. He and his people needed friends among the whites in order to obtain fair treatment in their new way of life.

Sitting Bull had another friend in Colonel Andrews, on whom he depended for help in the running of his camp, including procurement of extra food and new clothing. At the beginning of June, Andrews had sent an order off to the quartermaster depot for clothing and other supplies, but the colonel did not receive confirmation or acceptance of this order until 17 August.[31] If supplies arrived by the end of the month, three months would have lapsed between request and delivery. The delay must have prompted quite a few visits from Sitting Bull. Indeed, when Andrews looked out of his office window and saw the chief, with a small entourage of headmen, approaching his office, the commander might well have muttered to himself, "Here he comes again."

On one occasion, though, Andrews had to ask for Sitting Bull's help. In November 1881, Major McLaughlin of the Standing Rock Agency had written to Andrews about stolen property that belonged to the Hunkpapa chief, Long Soldier. Swift Cloud of Sitting Bull's band had stolen a large silver medal and some papers from Long Soldier when he was at Standing Rock, the major told Andrews. McLaughlin's letter was mislaid, and not until 29 July did Andrews reply, stating that he had asked Sitting Bull to look into this matter for him. Sitting Bull determined that Swift Cloud, who was not with the Hunkpapas at Fort Randall, had taken Long Soldier's wife away from him, and it was likely that she had taken the papers and medal with her. While it is not known if Long Soldier ever got his property back, he would not have been the first person to lose his valuables to a departing spouse.[32] More importantly, Andrews trusted Sitting Bull's assessment of the situation and allowed him to exercise his leadership.

FORT RANDALL,
AUGUST–OCTOBER 1882

The boredom that permeated the Hunkpapa camp for the men cannot be too strongly emphasized. They literally had nothing to do. For Sitting Bull, it was not so bad; he had visitors to break the monotony, and he also spent time in running the camp and maintaining order. Nevertheless, idle hours occurred for him as well. He filled some days with drawing and painting, and during his time at Fort Randall, he made three sets of pictographs of his war exploits against the Crows, Assiniboines, Arikaras, Flatheads, Gros Ventres, and Ojibwas. Unlike the previous war record that he had drawn for Jumping Bull, these drawings showed no events involving white men. Working in old ledger books, he used pencil, ink, and watercolors from a paintbox probably acquired from Daniel L. Pratt, Jr., the post trader, for whom the chief made the first set of drawings. This set is known as the Pettinger Record, named after Pratt's niece. Sitting Bull made the next set for Lieutenant Wallace Tear, First Lieutenant, Twenty-fifth Infantry, who acquired them for his benefactor, Brevet Brigadier General John C. Smith.[1] No doubt Sitting Bull asked the lieutenant for payment for this work of art. Sitting Bull had need of money and rarely did favors for white men, no matter how well he knew them. Tear wrote to Smith that he was trying to think of some trinket that he could give to Sitting Bull as a gift from the general, adding that it would not cost much.[2]

For the third set, however, Sitting Bull appears not to have made any request for payment. Captain Quimby's wife Martha had requested this set. She, her sister Margaret Smith, and her sister's daughters, eighteen-month-old Belle and five-year-old Alice, were frequent visitors in Sitting Bull's tipi. Alice was a particular favorite of the chief.

Charles Picotte. South Dakota State Historical Society

Rudolf Cronau. South Dakota State Historical Society

(opposite) White Swan. DeLancey Gill photograph,
South Dakota State Historical Society

Cronau's painting of Sitting Bull. South Dakota State Historical Society

(opposite) Thomas Tibbles.
Nebraska State Historical Society

Alice Fletcher. National Anthropological Archives, Smithsonian Institution

(opposite, top) Fletcher's sketch of Fort Randall. National Anthropological Archives, Smithsonian Institution

(opposite, bottom) Fletcher's sketch of Sitting Bull's camp. National Anthropological Archives, Smithsonian Institution

From Mrs Andrews, Cede married in Palie
Ft. Randall, Oct. 24. 1881.

Sitting Bull's first camp Ft. Randall
Oct. 1881.

Sitting Bull with members of his family and a visiting white woman and child at Fort Randall. Captain Bentzoni sits on his horse in the background. Bailey, Dix and Mead photograph, South Dakota State Historical Society

Three Hunkpapa women return to camp, carrying wood they have gathered.
Bailey, Dix and Mead photograph, South Dakota State Historical Society

Bishop Martin Marty. South Dakota State Historical Society

(opposite) R. L. Kelley's photograph of Sitting Bull.
South Dakota State Historical Society

Sitting Bull

R. L. Kelly,   Pierre, S. D.

Reverend John P. Williamson. South Dakota State Historical Society

When they visited they often brought gifts of food and other items for the family. On one of these visits, Martha Quimby had seen the chief working on the drawings for Lieutenant Tear and asked him if he could make some drawings for her. He agreed, and her set eventually consisted of thirteen drawings similar to those made previously, except for the last one, which was never finished.[3]

Friday, 4 August, could well have been one of those days when Sitting Bull was working on his drawings. For the other men, it was another uneventful day. While the women busied themselves, the men sat around smoking, reminiscing, and amusing themselves with games of chance. Suddenly the calm was shattered. Out of nowhere, an Indian on horseback and armed with a rifle galloped into the camp. Stopping at one of the tipis, he grabbed two young boys and galloped away. It happened so quickly that the camp guards did not have time to react. The Indian was White Dog, and the two boys were his sons, twelve-year-old Winter and nine-year-old Ran-Behind. White Dog got clean away. No soldiers followed him, for the simple reason that there were no mounted troops at the fort.[4] Andrews immediately sent letters to the respective agents, advising them of the abduction and requesting them to arrest White Dog and turn him over to the military.

The event must have been an embarrassment for Colonel Andrews. Receiving information that White Dog had been seen at the Rosebud Sun Dance, the colonel assumed that he would make his way to either the Rosebud or Pine Ridge agencies.[5] Andrews therefore wrote to the commanding officers at Forts Hale and Niobrara, requesting the officers to take charge of the Hunkpapa and his sons and hold them until their "final disposition can be determined by competent authority." Thinking of everything, Andrews closed the letters with the information that White Dog and his sons could be fed "under the provisions of General Orders No. 100, of Oct. 27, 1877." He commented to both commanders that White Dog was "a very ugly Indian."[6] Whether he was referring to his physical appearance or his demeanor is not known, although he had referred to him in an earlier letter as being "troublesome."[7] It depended on your point of view. White Dog had accepted into his family, as an adopted son, the severely crippled Shoshone-Bannock Indian called Steps, who had lost both feet and his right hand after a severe snowstorm.

While White Dog had liberated his sons, his wife The-Good-Nation-Woman, his nephew Black Prairie Chicken, his two daughters Eagle-Wing-Woman and The-Lodge-Behind with her son Killed, and, of course, Steps remained at Fort Randall.[9] With only one adult male left in the family to look after them, they would have needed the support of others in the camp, which, following Lakota tradition, would have been freely given. Being prisoners, they would not have to worry about food, and Sitting Bull, as chief of the band, would have made sure they did not go short of the necessities of life—that was part of being a Lakota chief.

In mid-August, a policy that the United States government had adopted in 1869 had a direct impact on Sitting Bull's Lakotas. In an attempt to alleviate corruption in treatment of American Indians, President Ulysses S. Grant had established his so-called Peace Policy, which provided for the education and training in industrial pursuits of Indian youths, both male and female. The Carlisle Indian Industrial School in Pennsylvania and the Hampton Normal and Agricultural Institute in Virginia became the flagships of this new approach. The regimens in these boarding schools were strict, and administrators did everything to obliterate the "Indianness" of their pupils, both mentally and physically. Most of the children adapted, but others did not, and their three-to-four-year-stays, without any interim visits back home, were hellish experiences.[10]

On 22 July 1882, the Office of Indian Affairs had informed the Secretary of the Interior that, of the Sioux youths to be sent to Carlisle that year, ten were to come from Sitting Bull's band at Fort Randall. Captain Richard H. Pratt, who was in charge of Carlisle, had made arrangements with Alice Fletcher for student transport. When she returned to Dakota Territory to continue her studies of the Indians, she would take charge of a group of thirty-eight students who were returning home. At the same time, she was to select fresh students from among the Indians she would be visiting, Sitting Bull's band included, and return with them in the fall.[11] Colonel Andrews would help her select ten children from among the Hunkpapas. This order of 22 July got caught up in the usual military bureaucracy. On 24 July, the Interior Department informed the Secretary of War, who, in turn, on 2 August, instructed the Commander-in-Chief of the Army, General Tecumseh Sherman, to inform the commanding general of the Military Division of the Missouri, Lieutenant General Sheridan, who on 7 August informed the commanding general of the Department of Dakota, General Terry, who finally informed Colonel Andrews on 9 August in a letter that he received on 11 August—twenty-one days after the initial order.[12]

The day before he got his official orders, Andrews had received a telegram from Pratt, asking the colonel to send the Hunkpapa children to Sioux City on 15 August, or, if that were not possible, Pratt would collect them himself in September when he gathered children from the Rosebud and Pine Ridge agencies. A few days earlier, Andrews had received a letter from Pratt in which he was informed that Miss Alice Fletcher would take eight children from Sitting Bull's camp to join the twenty children she would collect from the Omaha reservation in Nebraska. It would be difficult, within the time she had, to collect both groups, so he had requested that the children from Sitting Bull's camp be sent to Sioux City, Iowa, where they would join up with Fletcher and the Omaha children. Pratt preferred that both groups arrive at the school together. Andrews's reply, sent on 12 August, stated that he had no authorization to send the children to Sioux City, but that he would hand them over to Pratt when he arrived in September. He also pointed out that his orders called for ten children and not eight as specified by Pratt.[13]

Alice Fletcher was unaware of these communications. Arriving at Sioux City, she was alarmed to find no Hunkpapa children waiting for her. Making matters worse, she was unable to find out any news about them. She sent a telegram to Colonel Andrews on 12 August enquiring about the whereabouts of the missing Hunkpapa children. The colonel did not receive this telegram until the evening of 16 August, the day after she had been told to expect the children. The telegraph service was notoriously unreliable at Fort Randall. Andrews wrote back to her the next day, explaining that he had only just received her telegram and informing her that there was "great reluctance" to let any children go, even though Sitting Bull strongly advised the parents to agree. Andrews ventured the opinion that, as no decision had yet been made, in the end the Hunkpapas would comply.[14]

He was to be proved wrong. "I have had several interviews with Sitting Bull, and his people," he wrote to General Terry on 27 August,   103 "have also brought to bear upon them every influence at my command calculated to produce the desired result, but without avail, as their final decision was communicated to me today, as follows; 'If we were on a reservation we would let the children go, but as we are not, we cannot.'"[15] After all the councils, the majority of the Hunkpapas were against sending any of their children away to Carlisle. They may have agreed to send a few children across the river to school, but to send them so far away for three to four years was out of the question. Little Gertie Bell's death and burial away from her family was a clear indicator of what could happen. The "moccasin telegraph" would also have told them of the treatment their children could expect at Carlisle—hair cut short, forced to wear white man's clothes, and forbidden to speak their own language. Rumors of physical punishments meted out to children there shocked all the Hunkpapas. The illnesses and deaths at these boarding schools alarmed them. No doubt the Hunkpapas had heard that when the Brulé chief Spotted Tail visited Carlisle, he did not like what he saw. In spite of Pratt's bullying, Spotted Tail took his children back home.[16] Sitting Bull's band would not allow their offspring to go.

Colonel Andrews was sure that the Hunkpapas were using these objections as a lever to get them released from Fort Randall. In his annual report for the year ending 1 September 1882, the colonel indicated the thinking behind the resistance to Carlisle. The Hunkpapas were reasoning "that if the authorities can find time to dispose of ten children, it would take no more time to dispose of them all by locating them on a reservation."[17] Their resistance gave Andrews a new problem, however.

"As I understand the instructions of the General of the Army," the colonel wrote to his superior, "I shall upon his arrival, turn over to Lieut. Pratt, ten selected children, notwithstanding the objections of their parents, but if possible, please inform me, prior to the time for action, if my interpretation of the instructions given [by] the General of the Army is correct."[18] His request was forwarded to the War Department, who forwarded it to the Interior Department, who forwarded it to the commissioner of Indian affairs, who sent a copy of the letter to Pratt for his opinions on the matter. The commissioner reported back that Pratt said that "it is not well to do violence to the sentiments of the Indians on this question of education, and suggests that when he goes to Dakota after the Rosebud and Pine Ridge Sioux, he can visit Sitting Bull's people and perhaps put the matter before them in a very different light from that Col. Andrews is able to, he having very little knowledge of the school or the plans of the Department."[19] The commissioner agreed, and the letter ran up and down the chain of departmental command, eventually reaching Andrews on 10 October with instructions that no children were to be taken away to Carlisle without the consent of their parents—a small but significant victory for the Hunkpapas.[20]

As it turned out, Pratt never made it to Fort Randall. A four-week absence on departmental business in Arizona and Philadelphia had created a backlog of work at Carlisle that made it impossible for him to go to Dakota Territory to collect new students. In his place, he sent one of his teachers, a Miss Burgess, and three of his best Lakota pupils—Luther Standing Bear, Maggie Stands Looking, and Robert American Horse. They would act as interpreters for Miss Burgess, telling and showing what they had learned at Carlisle. With them as examples, the authorities hoped that more parents would allow their children to return east with them. "If after a full understanding from these," Pratt wrote to Andrews in October, "Sitting Bull still prefers not send his children we must let the matter drop as the Department does not want any children here except with the full consent of their people and parents."[21] These comments were unusually considerate for Captain Pratt, but then he was under orders. His attitude about the future of the Indian was radical. He advocated integrating them completely into white society, irrespective of what the Indians wanted. Anything connected to their traditional way of life, he zealously objected to, and he was not above using bully-boy tactics to get his way.[22]

Burgess and her three charges did make it to Fort Randall. With the help of the post interpreter, Burgess "had quite a little conversation" with Sitting Bull, but the three young Lakotas said little. It was all to no avail—no children went to Carlisle from the camp, and the matter was dropped. Although it would seem as if Sitting Bull himself were in favor of sending children to Carlisle, the colonel was probably correct in his assessment that the refusal was a political ploy on the chief's part. For the first time in his relatively brief dealings with the United States authorities, he had found it possible to defeat them if his people stuck together. Sitting Bull was sufficiently a realist to recognize that times had changed and that he and his people would have to go along with these changes, especially the younger people. As chief, he could try to make sure they had a good path to follow, and this success would feed his obstinacy toward any change that he considered bad for the future of his people. He had learned that it was possible to face up to the white man within their own system.

When Bishop William H. Hare wrote to Colonel Andrews on 28 August to ask if he should keep places open for some of the Hunkpapa children again that year at Saint Paul's and Saint Mary's, he had chosen a bad time to ask. The children who had been there for the previous term had impressed their teachers with their intelligence and behavior, and the bishop was now looking to accept four boys and two girls for the new term—an increase of one boy and a replacement for Gertie Bell. This letter arrived in the middle of discussions over Carlisle, and Andrews replied that the prospects of sending children to school again were "not very encouraging," but that he hoped that success might be possible within a few weeks.[25]

Bishop Hare stood a better chance of schooling a few Hunkpapa children than Pratt did. In his annual report, Andrews wrote that the young boys "are anxious to return to school, but the parents are unwilling, desiring to make their consent contingent upon the band being placed upon a reservation."[26] In the end, the boys won. In September, the Hunkpapas sent six boys across the river for a further term. However, no girls were sent to Saint Mary's, perhaps due to Gertie Bell's death, although the Hunkpapas may have acknowledged that she had been kindly treated. Although their names are not recorded, the six boys probably included the original three, Little Soldier, Charge-on-the-House, and Rock.[27]

At the beginning of September, two visitors had arrived at Fort Randall from Pine Ridge Agency—Episcopalian missionary John Robinson and George Sword. Sword, a nephew of the Oglala chief Red Cloud, was captain of the Pine Ridge Indian police and one of the most progressive leaders of the Sioux. On 5 September, Sword had a talk with Sitting Bull, during which he urged the chief to accept the wishes of the government and send children to school. Sitting Bull replied that he expected to go to see the president soon, and he would tell him what he wanted. The chief may have pinned his hopes on the petition that Bishop Marty and Major McLaughlin had engineered, which he had signed on 15 August.[28]

On 5 September, Colonel Andrews made his report to the Department of Dakota for the year ending 1 September 1882. Concerning his prisoners he reported:

> They have caused but very little trouble and thus far, their conduct has been commendable. The restrictions, necessarily imposed upon their freedom of movements, together with the uncertainty of their future, are to them a source of annoyance and anxiety.
>
> . . . Slight disagreements spring up among them at intervals, and in one case led to violence, but in no instance has it been necessary for the troops to use force to restore order.
>
> Since their arrival at the post, twelve have died. Viz: one of old age, one of scrofula, one of dropsey, one of pneumonia, six of consumption, one of Valular [sic] disease of the heart, and one female infant of acute diarrhea. These deaths, while it is evident, their causes in almost every instance originated prior to the arrival at the post, are working upon their superstitious natures, are much talked about among themselves, and in my interviews with them I find has materially increased of late, their anxiety, to be removed, "lest death should over take them all."

In the same report, Andrews recorded eight births since 1 April 1882. Most of these babies survived their stay at Fort Randall.[29]

In spite of their fears, the members of Sitting Bull's band were slowly coming to terms with their new lifestyle, which was totally dependent on the white man. Once a proud and independent people, they now had to ask for things from their old enemies. The Sioux, lions of the plains, had had their claws drawn. As another winter in captivity bore down upon them, the Lakotas once more had to beg help from Colonel Andrews. Their tipis were worn and rotten, the worse for the storms of the Plains, and would offer little protection during the coming winter. These were the tipis they had brought from Standing Rock, and some had probably come with them from Canada, making them three years old. The Hunkpapas, with no horses, no guns, and no buffalo herds in the vicinity, had no option but to ask the military to help them replenish their living quarters. The army had provided canvas as a substitute, but there was not enough of it. In mid-October, temporary commander of Fort Randall Captain Gaines Lawson estimated that the Hunkpapas needed canvas for another ten tipis. He had quite a number of canvas tents in storage at the fort, and although considerably worn, they would fill the gap. Accordingly, on 18 October, Lawson wrote to Major Breck seeking permission to give these tents to the Hunkpapas, stressing the fact that, with winter now so close, prompt action was needed to avoid bringing suffering to his charges. Permission was granted and received on the twenty-sixth. Within a few days, he would have released the canvas from the stores, and the Hunkpapa women would have busied themselves in making new tipi covers.[30]

That fall, Second Lieutenant George P. Ahern also arrived at Fort Randall. The twenty-two-year-old had recently graduated from West Point Military Academy and would become a good friend of Sitting Bull, who gave him the name of *Kahrinumpah* or "Two Crows." When the commanding officer learned that Ahern understood French and German, he appointed him to deal with Sitting Bull's correspondence. The chief received mail regularly from all over the world. The letters often asked for his autograph or a memento such as a pipe or his tomahawk.[31] This letter from France is probably typical of Sitting Bull's fan mail:

> I write you these few words to present to you my wishes of good friendship, and I desire that you live a long time.
> For I like you well and I am not telling you any lies.
> I am not lying and it's my heart that speaks. I have asked you for several curios from your country and you haven't sent any to me yet. I will pay you the price that you ask. Send me then a pipe which is not an impossible thing for you to do. When you write me tell me the names and the ages of your sons and yours also, if you please. Especially answer me if it be only a few words to prove to me that you are thinking of me. Waiting to read your letter and shake your hand cordially.
> Your friend who likes you
> Paul Richard[32]

It is doubtful if Monsieur Richard got the pipe, for Sitting Bull had learned to get his money up front. He received many requests by letter for his autograph, but he only complied if a dollar were enclosed. This income enabled him to buy luxuries, such as paints and tobacco, from the post trader. Ahern wrote Sitting Bull's responses to the letters to which the chief chose to reply.[33]

Ahern made daily visits to Sitting Bull, and the chief would often make return calls to the officer's quarters. On one of the lieutenant's early visits, quite probably his first, he left his calling card. Sitting Bull no doubt puzzled over the exchange until he learned about the white man's custom of leaving a card with his name on it when he called. Sitting Bull wrote his name on the back of this card, and when he next visited Ahern, "with a smile and twinkle in his eye," he left the card on a table. After Ahern attended to the business of Sitting Bull's mail, he and the chief would chat like old friends. They discussed the merits of horses, which were of interest to them both, and Sitting Bull would reminisce about hunting and traveling across the Plains in his days of freedom, although he never spoke of his war exploits.[34]

Ahern also attended meetings that Sitting Bull had with Sioux chiefs who came from various parts of the Great Sioux Reservation, usually in groups of five or six, to pay their respects and ask his advice. The lieutenant was "tremendously impressed" with the great respect these men showed towards the Hunkpapa chief. They would talk of old friends, of their new way of life, and of events from the old nomadic life. From them, Sitting Bull would learn of what was happening at the agencies, of the dealings with agency officials, of the difficulties of farming and raising cattle on poor land. At the same time, the chief was educating a young and callow Ahern, who recalled that he had "made a 'break'" in the first conference:

As the pipe passed slowly from one to another in the group squatting in a circle in Sitting Bull's tepee, it came to me. I hesitated a moment, and then said to Sitting Bull, "I have never smoked, and do not wish to begin now." It was rather foolish but Sitting Bull promptly replied, "Good, if you do not smoke you will keep a good eye and a good nerve." Rather good for an Indian, but I was getting such jolts of wisdom daily from this man.

From this close contact I learned to admire him for his wisdom, his unswerving loyalty to his people, and his frank critical attitude towards the whites in authority over his people.[35]

The young lieutenant also saw a good deal of Sitting Bull's children and became good friends with five-year-old Stands Holy. When he walked through the camp, she would accompany him, holding his hand. Ahern became so attached to her that he asked her father to let him send her to a convent school in Saint Louis. Ahern wrote later, "The little girl came to my side, took my hand, and looked as if she would like to go, but her father said 'No, I love her too much. Nothing but sorrow would come of it.'"[36]

Sitting Bull was a good family man, and his children were his pride and joy. His youngest was now just over a year old, and he had named her Sallie Battles, after Colonel Andrews's young niece who had visited the camp. Being the youngest child in the chief's family, Sallie received plenty of attention. "The baby was very ill and had several convulsions while I was present," Ahern recalled later. "After one severe convulsion, when it looked as if the end was near, Sitting Bull took hold of its little wrist to feel the pulse, and imagine my amazement to see the tears rolling down his cheeks, and he [was] actually sobbing. Here was one supposed to be a hard-hearted savage displaying emotions that we all thought the Indian warrior scorned—tears—and sobbing like a woman. The baby died the following morning at daybreak."[37]

Sitting Bull was no stranger to the death of his children. His first child, aged four, had died in 1857. In 1876, one of his twin sons, born the previous year and the brother of Crowfoot, died when he was kicked in the head by a horse. In 1877, a nine-year-old-son died of disease.[38] Each loss was a sadness that the chief never forgot, and this last, coming in the depths of the second winter of confinement, must have deepened his anxiety for the future of his family and his people.

FORT RANDALL,
NOVEMBER 1882–JANUARY 1883

Back on 25 September, Colonel Andrews had gone on leave for six months, with permission to take an extra six months if he wanted to. This action left Captain Gaines Lawson, Twenty-fifth Infantry, in charge as acting commanding officer. On 3 November, Lawson received a telegram, addressed to the commanding officer, instructing the Twenty-fifth Infantry Regiment to leave Fort Randall; the Fifteenth Infantry Regiment would replace them. Captain Lawson may well have expressed a few kind words about the colonel being on leave at such a time. In fairness, Andrews would have had no prior knowledge of this move, and from the telegrams sent from the headquarters of the Department of Dakota, they do not appear to have realized that he was on official leave. In any case, Lawson coped with the situation, and the transfer went off with only one minor mishap. A soldier from F Company, named Corporal White, refused to leave without his half-breed wife and deliberately stayed behind, disobeying the orders of his company commander, Captain H. Baxter Quimby.[1]

Lieutenant George Ahern probably received the responsibility of telling Sitting Bull about the transfer, although Captain Lawson may have been present. Just as the Hunkpapas had become used to the Buffalo Soldiers and they in turn had gotten used to the Hunkpapas, the military decided to change things around. Sitting Bull had had a good working relationship with Colonel Andrews, and vice versa. The colonel had the rare distinction of being one of the few white men in authority that Sitting Bull trusted, and he, in return, learned to respect this Lakota chief who showed so much concern for the welfare of his band. Two questions uppermost in the minds of all those in the Hunkpapa camp

111

were, what would the new soldier chief be like? and would these white soldiers be as friendly as the Buffalo Soldiers? Another set of uncertainties had entered life at Fort Randall.

On the morning of 17 November, the headquarters, band, and Companies B and I of the Twenty-fifth Infantry left Fort Randall on the Steamer *General Terry*. Even at the early hour, the Hunkpapas would have gone to the river bank to watch as their old guardians left. The troops were to travel the short distance to Running Water, where they would continue their journey to Fort Snelling by rail.[2] Also leaving on the steamer was Lieutenant Ahern, who had already said his good-byes to the family of Sitting Bull. The lieutenant was saddened at leaving a man he had come to respect and like. "I always felt the utmost confidence in Sitting Bull," Ahern wrote years later, "and would have willingly gone to him had he gone on the war path and would have felt safe at approaching him at any time."[3] In 1929, after retiring with the rank of major, Ahern received an invitation from General Charles J. Summerall of the War Department to attend a luncheon at which Red Tomahawk, one of the two policemen who killed Sitting Bull in 1890, was to be a guest. Ahern politely refused to attend—such was his lasting respect for his old friend.[4]

On 19 November, the *General Terry* returned with the new soldiers who would be in charge of Sitting Bull and his band. Under the command of Lieutenant Colonel Peter T. Swaine, the headquarters, band, and Companies C and D of the Fifteenth Infantry disembarked. As soon as they were ashore, the remaining two companies of the Twenty-fifth Infantry, Companies F and G, embarked for their journey to Running Water, and then on to Forts Snelling and Hale by rail. One of the friends that Sitting Bull was losing that day was the family of Captain Quimby. With the sudden departure, the chief was unable to complete the drawings of his war exploits that he had promised to Martha Quimby. The last drawing was of a horse, but he had not had time to add human figures. Just before the boat left, Sitting Bull handed the ledger to Mrs. Quimby, apologizing that he had not had time to finish the last drawing. He and the Hunkpapas watched from the riverbank as the steamer pulled away from the fort.[5]

The remaining Fifteenth Infantry companies, A and H, arrived belatedly at Fort Randall on 4 December. The soldiers had transferred from Colorado at a really unsuitable time. They were used to relatively mild winters in comparison to the extremes of Dakota Territory. Ever since his arrival at Fort Randall, Lieutenant Colonel Swaine had been concerned with problems that the move to the new post had created for the welfare of his men. When the regiment arrived, they did not have suitable clothing. The men found that they now needed arctic overshoes, heavy quality trousers, and woolen blankets. Swaine had much correspondence with the Department of Dakota over the situation. The weather did not help, making transportation of goods and rations difficult.[6] There were other problems as well:

> The duties of the water detail (changed daily) are most laborious—all the water for this large post is dipped by the single bucket from the river half a mile distant by road, transferred to a tank and distributed in like primitive manner into barrels. The water freezes as it enters and flows from the tank, the buckets and clothing of the men become covered with ice, and in some instances the men themselves have become frostbitten. Constant labor for the whole of these short days often leave us with an insufficiency of water, and to interupt this service, would still further diminish the supply, while it is doubtful if practical benefit could be obtained in the effort to [illegible] men coming in with wet and frozen clothing, and so much fatigued. Guard is next in order, as an arduous duty, with over 150 Indian Prisoners, and scattered stores etc it requires a daily detail of 4 N.C. Officers and 15 privates for this duty. Sentinels are exposed to extreme degrees of low temperature, the guardhouse is so small that part of the guard have to occupy room with the prisoners, besides it is a barren place with door open most of the time to hear calls of sentinels posting reliefs, etc.— too uncomfortable in fact to require men to remove overclothing for a setting up and other drills.[7]

The cold affected the Hunkpapas, too, but they were used to it. Their snug tipis, now repaired and emitting a warm glow from their fires, would have been the envy of the soldier guards as they patrolled the camp in the freezing cold.

Apart from their skin color, the Hunkpapas saw no difference between the soldiers of the Fifteenth and Twenty-fifth Infantry. The guards were friendly enough, and new friendships developed between the officers and their families and the Lakotas. There was one difference, though; alcohol use increased. Sitting Bull detested the white man's whiskey. He had seen the demoralizing effect it had on some of the Sioux who chose to live near the military and fur-trading forts. Colonel Andrews had held the same view, and during his time at Fort Randall, the post trader, John Cunningham, was prohibited from selling intoxicating liquor. No doubt, the ordinary soldier had ways of obtaining liquor, but the Buffalo Soldiers had, by far, the lowest rates of alcoholism in the United States Army.[8] Lieutenant Colonel Swaine had different ideas. When the post trader applied for permission to sell alcoholic drinks, Swaine "most earnestly recommended" his application.[9]

Whether the application was ultimately successful is not known, but alcohol was available. One source was company H's Chinese cook, Edward Day Cohota, who was a keen gambler and something of a bootlegger. Denny Moran, who was a civilian driver for the regimental headquarters, wrote in his reminiscences that "Ka Hote" offered him fifty dollars to get five gallons of whiskey, with an additional twenty dollars for smuggling it into the fort. This arrangement was the first of several importations of whiskey in which the pair were involved. Officers had other arrangements with Moran, who brought in small quantities of hard liquor for their own private consumption. Yankton, across and down the river, could have been another source of supply for both men and officers, but soldiers were not generally welcome there.[10]

On 21 November, two visitors arrived at the fort to stay with the Hunkpapas. Little Assiniboine, also known as Jumping Bull, and Gray Eagle had ridden down from Fort Yates with a pass from Major James McLaughlin, but the two men had to be back at Standing Rock Agency by 8 December, giving them about ten days to spend with their relatives. They were something of an odd couple to travel together. Jumping Bull was the adopted brother of Sitting Bull, who had saved him from death in 1857 when Jumping Bull had been captured in a fight between the Lakotas and the Assiniboines. Although only about thirteen years old, the young Assiniboine had put up a defiant fight, and the Lakota warriors were all for killing him. Sitting Bull intervened, adopted him as his brother, and gave him the name of his late father, Jumping Bull—a great honor. He lived up to the name, becoming a distinguished warrior who was faithful to his Hunkpapa brother until they died together in the same incident in 1890.[11]

Gray Eagle, on the other hand, was Sitting Bull's brother-in-law and had been with him on many war expeditions, but the two men had fallen out in Canada. As headman, Sitting Bull had punished Gray Eagle when he and Pretty Crow had stolen horses from the Crees. The Redcoats had arrested Gray Eagle and asked Sitting Bull whether they should punish him or if Sitting Bull wished to inflict punishment according to Sioux custom. Sitting Bull decided to attend to the issue himself and had a group of *akicitas* take Gray Eagle to the top of a high butte, where he was told to gallop down the butte on horseback. If he reached the bottom without mishap, he would be set free, but if he failed, he was to "die the penalty of death." Gray Eagle was successful, but the affair tarnished the relationship between the two brothers-in-law.[12] While they were by no means enemies, they did have opposing views on their new lifestyle. Gray Eagle was one of the first ex-hostiles to take up farming, wear white man's clothes, and become a strong advocate of reservation life. Sitting Bull was one of the last.[13]

The days this unlikely pair spent with their relatives were full of feasting and gossiping. The Hunkpapas were eager for the latest news of their relatives at Standing Rock. Sitting Bull was no doubt dismayed to learn that his old lieutenants, Gall and Crow King, who had adapted to reservation life, had been allowed to go to a fair in Minneapolis, while he was stuck at Fort Randall. The men would also have discussed the proposed selling of part of the land that comprised the Great Sioux Reservation, a proposal to which Sitting Bull was opposed. Both Jumping Bull and Gray Eagle had been present when talks with the Standing Rock Sioux had started about 15 November, but they would not have made it back for the signing of the agreement on 30 November.[14]

This plan had first seen the light of day on 20 February 1882, when Richard F. Pettigrew, the congressional delegate for Dakota Territory, introduced a bill into the House of Representatives, proposing that the northern part of the reservation, above the "White Earth," should be opened for settlement.[15] The *Bismarck Tribune* of 2 June 1882 carried an explanation: the Great Sioux Reservation was "in the heart of the territory of Dakota, and is as large or larger than the great state of New York, and includes a vast area of valuable agricultural and grazing lands, equal to any in the world, and is surrounded by growing and prosperous communities; on the west by the Black Hills counties, which, in addition to their agricultural resources are the seat of the richest mineral deposits in the whole country."[16]

At a meeting held in Deadwood, in the heart of the Black Hills, miners and town boosters passed the following resolution: "That the right of the Indians to the reservation should be extinguished absolutely and speedily (to all save a reasonable area for their actual occupancy), and every interest which is worthy of consideration, appeals to congress in behalf of this result. The growing demands of the people, stimulated by the advanced tide of unprecedented immigration demand it." The resolution passed unanimously and was forwarded to the secretary of the interior and the commissioner of Indian affairs.[17] The people of Bismarck and Deadwood were only voicing the opinions of the majority of the people in the western states and territories, and direct pressure on the Indians to cede part of the Great Sioux Reservation was not long in coming.

On 11 July, Pettigrew made a speech to the House of Representatives concerning his proposed bill, which proffered some more strong opinions:

Within a year past the bloodthirsty Sitting Bull, with his band of murderers, returned to the United States from Canada and they have taken up their domicile upon the reservation, where they, too, as well as the others, are supported at government expense in vagabondage and idleness.

These people are gathered at five different points in the reservation, where there are government agencies established, at which points the different bands have fixed their homes, and where the women and children are fed and protected while the warriors are abroad marauding and pillaging. No white person is permitted to enter on any portion of this vast domain, even in search of strayed stock, under penalty of arrest and imprisonment by the government authorities, although there are extensive portions within the reservation never visited by the Indians themselves, there being no game to allure them. There are exceptions to this exclusion of white persons. Those who debase themselves to cohabit with Indian squaws and conform to their customs, are permitted to become of their number and reside among them.[18]

What might Major McLaughlin have thought of the comment "debase themselves to cohabit with Indian squaws"? His wife's grandmother was a Mdewakanton Dakota who had married a Scottish fur trader. As for the Sioux warriors "marauding and pillaging," they were in fact all living peacefully on the reservation. The only Indian trouble on the Northern Great Plains came from the Blackfeet and Crees crossing over the border from Canada.[19] Self-interest, and not reality, was driving this debate.

Pettigrew's bill was added to the Sundry Civil Appropriations Bill, which passed on 7 August, authorizing negotiations with the Sioux in order to modify existing treaties. Secretary of the Interior Henry M. Teller established the Sioux Land Commission to visit the agencies and find out if the Indians were willing to sell any of their lands. The man chosen to head this commission was Newton Edmunds of Yankton, who had been governor of Dakota Territory during the Civil War and had negotiated with the Sioux on other occasions. He now led a three-man commission, which also consisted of an ex-chief justice of the territorial supreme court, Peter Shannon, and the secretary of the interior's brother, James H. Teller. Reverend Samuel D. Hinman, a missionary, went along as interpreter. This commission formulated its own policy, proposing to split the reservation into six separate reservations based around the existing agencies of Cheyenne River, Crow Creek, Lower Brulé, Pine Ridge, Rosebud, and Standing Rock. The surplus land would be sold, on the Indians' behalf, and opened up for settlement. What they did not tell the Sioux was that this surplus land would encompass almost half the existing Great Sioux Reservation. Even so, the Fort Laramie Treaty of 1868 required that three-quarters of all adult males sign any treaties or agreements involving land cessions. The committee had its work cut out for it.[20]

The commission left Yankton on 16 October and visited the Pine Ridge and Rosebud agencies before reaching Standing Rock in mid-November. They met strong opposition to their proposals wherever they went and produced, in spite of bullying tactics, a list of 384 signatures—a fraction of the number required by law (the adult male population on the Great Sioux Reservation was then about five thousand). A second effort the following year, headed by Hinman, would prove no more successful, and Congress would not approve the agreement. For the time being, the matter would be dropped.

Jumping Bull, Gray Eagle, and other visitors would have told Sitting Bull about the commission's visit to the various agencies, and Sitting Bull may have counseled them to stiffen their opposition to the selling of any lands, but he could not make his opinions known directly to the land commission even though it was based at Yankton. During Sitting Bull's time at Fort Randall, the commission made no attempt to meet with the chief. Edmunds probably considered the small band of Hunkpapa prisoners of war too insignificant to warrant his attentions. He may well have known about Sitting Bull's attitude toward the selling off of lands and decided not, as it were, to lock horns with the chief.

Three days after the Sioux Land Commission arrived at Standing Rock, an event took place that caused much talk among the Hunkpapas at Fort Randall—the hanging of Brave Bear. He was not a member of Sitting Bull's band, being a Yanktonai Sioux, but he had lived with them since he had joined them in Canada some time during the latter half of 1879. Brave Bear had murdered three men near Pembina in northeastern Dakota Territory in 1873 or 1874. He was caught and held in confinement at several locations for six months awaiting his trial, eventually escaping from the jail in Pembina. On the run, he stayed at different Sioux agencies, where his conduct was so obnoxious to the Lakotas that he was forced to keep moving on. In May 1879, he robbed and killed an ex-soldier, Joseph Johnson, which eventually led him to take refuge with the hostiles in Canada. Brave Bear had surrendered with Sitting Bull's Hunkpapas in 1881, although he had taken no part in any of the battles fought in 1876. At Standing Rock, he had learned that the new agent, already on his way to the agency, was to be James A. McLaughlin, who had played significant roles in his first arrest and second pursuit. Brave Bear absconded from Sitting Bull's camp the day before the band left for Fort Randall, leaving behind his wife and possibly a child.[21]

Although he slipped away from Sitting Bull's camp at Fort Yates, Brave Bear was soon arrested and sent to Yankton to await trial for the murder of Johnson. The trial commenced in early January 1882, and he was found guilty and sentenced to death by hanging, but due to several postponements, the sentence was not carried out until 16 November. During his trial, Brave Bear claimed to be Sitting Bull's son-in-law, which he may have thought would help his case. It did not, neither with the military nor with Sitting Bull. Brave Bear was everything that Sitting Bull despised—a thief who dressed in white man's fancy clothes and drank hard liquor. As no help was forthcoming from Sitting Bull, Brave Bear thereafter always denounced the chief in the "most emphatic and vulgar terms."[22] Strangely enough, both McLaughlin and Bishop Marty endeavored to have Brave Bear's sentence commuted to a term of imprisonment, giving as their reason that, among the Sioux, killing and stealing had been looked upon as acts of bravery. This defense distorted the honor system of the Lakotas, in which the act of stealing horses had as much to do with the dangers involved as with the accumulation of horse wealth. Killing earned a lower honor than counting coup (the striking of an armed and fighting enemy), which was a much more dangerous act. In this instance, the Lakotas would have seen Brave Bear as a murderer, not a warrior, and so might have condoned the sentence.[23]

When Brave Bear's trial started in November, Sitting Bull was no doubt annoyed that one of the two interpreters, who was also a witness, was none other than "Fish" Allison, who kept well away from Fort Randall. How the government could ignore his unsavory reputation and continue to have any dealings with him, let alone employ him, was a mystery. Allison and Brave Bear were two of a kind. At the time of his arrest, Brave Bear was carrying a card, signed by Allison, that entitled him to whiskey.[24] The final words on Brave Bear, though, belonged to his father, an honest and respectable man who when told by McLaughlin that his son was dead said, "We are glad, his mother and myself, for he was a bad son."[25]

After Allison had been forced to leave Fort Randall back in November 1881, an unknown and not particularly good interpreter had replaced him. J. B. Hassett, the post trader at White Swan, in June

1882 had informed Bishop Marty that Sitting Bull and his people were unsettled over the fact that no progress was being made towards their release from Fort Randall and that Colonel Andrews was not being kept informed about their feelings because "that clown of an interpreter [was] afraid to tell what they desire."[26] Lieutenant Colonel Swaine set about acquiring a new interpreter. Charles Picotte from the Yankton Agency presented him with two affidavits of his suitability for the post. Agent William Ridpath of the Yankton Agency called him "reliable and trustworthy" and stated that he had been a satisfactory interpreter at the agency.[27] The second affidavit, from a Mr. Smith at the Yankton Agency, was equally laudatory and added that Picotte had also been a member of the Indian police at the agency. Towards the end of December, Picotte got the job.[28]

Picotte was the stepson of Matilda Galpin, also known as Eagle Woman, whose first husband had been the Fort Pierre trader Honoré Picotte. The younger Picotte had already done some interpreting for Sitting Bull, although not in the capacity of official post interpreter. Sitting Bull knew that he could trust the stepson of Eagle Woman to interpret his words and wishes correctly. Mrs. Galpin had in fact sent a letter to Picotte via the boat that brought the Hunkpapas to Fort Randall, saying that she believed the chief would not cause any trouble and would keep his people "quiet and obedient." She wanted Charlie to impress upon Sitting Bull the fact that his conduct at the fort would dictate his future.[29]

Sitting Bull was as much concerned about the domestic affairs of his camp as he was about obtaining action on their future. Timber in the vicinity of the fort was almost nonexistent, due to the approved contractors who had cut down all the trees for miles around. The women of the camp had thus to go quite a distance to collect fuel for their families, with the added hardship of carrying it back to camp. One woman was already complaining of a sore back. Collecting wood was still woman's work—Lakota domestic life had not changed all that much. Sitting Bull was well aware of the problem and had registered the complaint with the colonel, asking for a wagon to ease the women's work, but it was not forthcoming. In the beginning of January, he asked Lieutenant Colonel Swaine for permission to buy, from across the river, a horse to work with a cart. He did not care how poor the horse was, he explained, as long as it was capable of doing the work intended. The head of the finest light cavalry in the world and a distinguished leader of horse-raiding expeditions was pleading to buy just one horse. Times had indeed changed. The colonel endorsed Sitting Bull's request in a letter sent to his superiors in the Department of Dakota, adding that the horse could be kept in the post interpreter's stable. General Terry agreed that something had to be done to help the women, but he preferred that, if it were possible, the post teams be used. Whether the Hunkpapas got a horse or the troops brought the wood into camp is not known, but either way, the chief had seen that the work was made a little lighter for the women.[30]

On 30 January 1883, Sitting Bull, in the company of Brave Thunder, High Bull, Fur (Hairy) Coat, and Charging Bear came to see Lieutenant Colonel Swaine with yet another problem. In the confusion of the move from Fort Yates to Fort Randall, the wives of these men had been left behind. From information the chief had received from Jumping Bull and Gray Eagle, as well as from other letters and recent visits from some Yanktonais Sioux, the husbands had learned that other men had now taken these women as wives. Gall had married one, and Sitting White Buffalo had taken another. The whereabouts of the other two were unknown, although Sitting Bull was sure that agent McLaughlin could find them. He wanted Swaine to write to his superiors to ensure that these women were released from their present partners and protected until they could be reunited with their husbands. He also wanted these men punished, as they would have been under Lakota tribal law, but that did not exist any more. The same day that Sitting Bull told Swaine about the missing wives, the colonel wrote to the Department of Dakota giving details of the situation. By the time the news traveled to McLaughlin (who replied two months later that the four women were well and only one had remarried), General Terry had advised Lieutenant Colonel Swaine that Sitting Bull's release was now imminent and the issue would sort itself out.[31] Two months would bring an enormous difference in Sitting Bull's circumstances.

RELEASE FROM
FORT RANDALL

Ever since Sitting Bull had arrived at Fort Randall, he had bombarded every white man or woman of any influence that he met with requests for help in having his band reunited with their kinsmen and friends at Standing Rock. His initial requests were simply for information about what was to happen to them, but later he pressed for release. It was not just post commanders Andrews and Swaine that he asked for help. Government officials received the first independent request for Sitting Bull's release in a letter from Rudolf Cronau to Hiram Price, the commissioner of Indian affairs, on 27 December 1881. The artist requested copies of the commissioner's reports for 1879 and 1881 so that he could complete several articles on the Indians of the West. Written before he had mastered English, the letter continued:

> I had occasion, to stay some weeks with Sitting Bull, which intelligent chief asked [me], to speak for him and his interests, what I did in a article, which will be published in the next time with the picture of Sitting Bull. He is very anxious, that the Great Father will allow him to come to Washington, so that it is possible for him to tell personally his wishes and willings, because he means, that agents and interpreters did not report, what he earnestly is willing to do. He asked [me] to tell the "Great father," that he likes to live as a white man, that he will send his children to the scool, and that he likes to have in the next spring a farm with cattle, good to support him and his family, there he likes not to receive the rations of the government. I found him as a man worth to speak for him and I hope that you will take his wishes into consideration.[1]

Whether a copy of this letter was forwarded to the War Department, under whose control Sitting Bull and his band had been placed, is not known. The letter was filed, but no action was taken.

A year later, the last independent request for Sitting Bull's release was sent to Washington in December 1882. Yankton chief Strike-the-Ree wrote an eloquent appeal:

> I am the Head Chief of the Yankton Sioux Indians. I am nearly eighty years old—was a man of war when I was young, and helped the Americans fight their enemies in seven battles. But I am an old man. I am a man of peace now. And I have a heart to pity the poor and unfortunate.
>
> So now I lift my voice and speak to you about Sitting Bull, whom you hold as a prisoner of war. My friend, for you are my friend, what has Sitting Bull been convicted of doing that you hold him a prisoner for so many long moons. I have always been told that our Grand Father was just and that he was generous. Tell me my friend when Sitting Bull was tried and condemned and I will say no more. I speak for him because he is kept in prison just across the river from me, and his moaning cry comes to my ear. There is no one else to speak for him so I plead his cause. The Americans know I am their friend and they ought to hear my words.
>
> So now my friend I know you have the power to do as you please, but I want you to think of this matter and do what is right. And I want you to tell me what you are going to do.
>
> And now my friend while I am writing I want to know if you have any of the neck ornaments moon shaped that the Government Officers once distributed to the Indian Head Soldiers. I want two for my head soldiers.
>
> My friend I shake your hands with a good heart.[2]

The letter was sent to the secretary of war, Robert T. Lincoln, who duly forwarded it to the secretary of the interior, Henry M. Teller, and the commissioner of Indian affairs, Hiram Price. In a letter accompanying Strike-the-Ree's request, Lincoln said that he agreed with the chief's views and hoped that funds could be made available from Congress that would enable the Indian Bureau to take control of Sitting Bull and his band at the beginning of the next fiscal year.[3] Some have claimed that this letter prompted the government to take action over Sitting Bull's future. If so, it must have been the only time that the United States Government had ever listened to the pleas of an old Indian chief. The letter raises the question, why would Strike-the-Ree, a "friendly" Indian, and one who had never ridden with the hostiles, take up the cause of the acknowledged leader of the hostile Sioux? The Reverend John Williamson wrote the letter for the chief, which prompts another question, how much of it is Williamson's opinion and how much is Strike-the-Ree's? Williamson had been making requests for the settlement of Sitting Bull's future ever since the chief had arrived at Randall, and he may have instigated the letter in the hopes that this approach would succeed where others had failed.[4]

All the previous letters concerning Sitting Bull's release that federal officials had received from Bishop Martin Marty, Reverend John Williamson, post commanders Andrews and Swaine, among others, were at last having an effect. The letter writers had repeatedly told of the chief's change of heart and his good conduct since becoming a prisoner of war.[5] To their names can be added that of Major James McLaughlin. He was able to point out to the authorities that the ex-hostiles under his care had settled down to reservation life, and even leaders such as Gall and Crow King had totally accepted their new circumstances.[6] To have Sitting Bull farming and living a Christian life on his reservation would be a large feather in the agent's cap.

At the beginning of January 1883, McLaughlin took a leave of absence from Standing Rock. He was away for forty-nine days, twenty-four of which he spent in Washington, D.C., negotiating Sitting Bull's return to Standing Rock. No doubt he had several informal meetings with various officials, culminating in a formal letter to the commissioner of Indian affairs. Writing from the Interior Department on 15 February, McLaughlin put forth the case for releasing the prisoners at Fort Randall:

I have the honor to state that "Sitting Bull" who is now held by the Military at Fort Randall D.T., as a prisoner of War, has applied to me several times during the past year, for intercession in his behalf, and that he with his people who are prisoners with him be transferred to the Interior Department and located on the Grand River at the Standing Rock Agency in Dakota.

I am now informed that the Military Authorities have no objections to such transfer, and as the Indians of the Standing Rock Agency are closely related to the Sitting Bull prisoners, they are very willing to aid them by sharing their supplies and assist in planting next spring. I would therefore respectfully suggest, if it is the intention of the Indian Department to place these Indians at the Standing Rock Agency, the propriety of sending them up the Missouri River, by one of the first boats in the Spring, which would be about the middle of April next, and which would enable them to plant some crops the coming season, thus placing them as not entirely dependent upon subsistence issues by the Government, should their arrival at the Agency, be delayed later than the first week in May there would be a whole year lost, before they could do anything toward helping themselves.

In view of these facts, and having the utmost confidence in the good intentions of Sitting Bull, I would respectfully recommend early action in bringing about the transfer of these people.[7]

McLaughlin wisely concentrated on two points. First, he argued that Sitting Bull was no longer a threat, and second (and equally important to officialdom), he pointed out that it would not cost much money to get these people to adapt to reservation life if everyone acted quickly.

The wheels of freedom were at last in motion. On 21 February, Price wrote to Teller, stating that he fully agreed with the contents of McLaughlin's letter. He suggested contacting the War Department to see if they could provide "transportation and subsistence" for the Hunkpapa prisoners and cover their needs for four weeks after their arrival at Standing Rock. If agreement on these points could be reached, he suggested a transfer date of about 15 April.[8] On 23 February, Teller wrote to Lincoln, stating that he was in agreement with the opinions of McLaughlin and Price. When the prisoners reached Standing Rock, the Interior Department would take over responsibility from the War Department and would provide for their location in the Grand River country. Teller stressed the importance, of acting on this release as quickly as possible so that Sitting Bull's band could be settled in their new location in time for spring planting.[9] On 15 March, Lincoln informed Teller that "the necessary orders" would be given for the release of Sitting Bull as requested.[10] Two days later, the adjutant general at the War Department, Brigadier General Richard C. Drum, wrote to the commanding general of the Military Division of the Missouri: "I have the honor to inform you that the Secretary of War directs that Sitting Bull and his party now held as prisoners of War at Fort Randall be sent to the Standing Rock Agency and there turned over to the Indian Agent who will be instructed to receive them."[11]

The order filtered its way through the proper military channels to Lieutenant Colonel Swaine, who received it on 26 March.[12] One assumes that he walked over to the Hunkpapa camp to give Sitting Bull the news the chief had waited for so long, although there is no record of it. Of course, the news would not have come as a total surprise to the Hunkpapas. The *Yankton Daily Press and Dakotaian* had reported on 21 March that Sitting Bull's release was imminent, giving a date of 15 April. The news would have wafted across the river into the Hunkpapa camp, courtesy of the chief's many visitors. Up north, McLaughlin would have heard about the order for Sitting Bull's release at about the same time as the chief did. Independent of each other, the two men sprang into action.[13]

In the middle of April, McLaughlin left the agency for a week to look over the Grand River country for a suitable site for the chief's new home. It was in this area that Sitting Bull had been born on the south bank of the river, at a place the Lakotas called Many Caches.[14] In mid-April, as well, Sitting Bull asked Lieutenant Colonel Swaine to write out a list of the chiefs and headmen of his band, as follows:

Sitting Bull	Chief
Red Thunder	Old chief, (1st)
Tall as the Cloud	Headman
The Man That Takes The Gun Away	" "
Looking Back Bear	Chief (2nd)
Young Red Thunder	" "
Mad Dog	"
Bone Tomahawk	" Head soldier #1

White Slow Buffalo	{ " "
	{whom S.B. wants as chief
Brave Thunder	Chief
Four Horns	" (oldest chief)
Fire Cloud	"
One Hand	" Head soldier
One Bull (nephew}	Head of police
Black Prairie Chicken	Head soldier, policeman
Standing Kill	" " "
Yellow Dog	Soldier
Standing Cloud	Head soldier (chief)
Roan Faced Bear	Chief soldier
Big Legs	Headman
His Holy Pipe	Soldier
Iron Heart	"
Four Horns, Jr.	"
Fur [Hairy] Coat	"

At the close of the letter, Swaine wrote: "The above list is made by the Post Commander at the urgent request of Sitting Bull, so that same can be presented to, and their respective status be confirmed by their Agent."[15]

Sitting Bull worried about Red Thunder, a displaced Minneconjou Lakota chief, who now wanted to return to his own people and have his status recognized accordingly. Sitting Bull "took a great interest in this matter," Swaine noted, and both chiefs "urgently requested" that McLaughlin be made aware of Red Thunder's wishes. Accordingly, Swaine had his adjutant write to McLaughlin with this information. Presumably, the agent later arranged for the Minneconjou to rejoin his people.[16]

On 8 April, Sitting Bull had also had a meeting with Lieutenant Colonel Swaine concerning the six boys away at Saint Paul's. He wanted to be sure that arrangements were made for their return to their families before they left for Standing Rock. Accordingly, Swaine's adjutant, First Lieutenant George Kinzie, Fifteenth Infantry, was ordered to inform the agent at Yankton, William Ridpath, to have the boys ready for return to Fort Randall. The colonel would telegraph the agent when the time came to send the boys over the river to join their parents on the boat.[17] Of these boys, Bishop William Hare wrote in his annual report for 1883:

> Six boys from the captive band of Sitting Bull have been in St. Paul's School during the past year, an addition of three to the number who were there last year from that band. It sets one to thinking, the fact that there were no six boys in the school quicker to learn, more tractable and more ready to coalesce with the general life of the school than this group fresh from the wildest Indian life, which had spurned the control of the Government, and asked only the privilege of ceaseless hunting and roaming. How hard it is sometimes to square our theories with our facts![18]

For the return of the Hunkpapas, the government chartered Captain Grant Marsh's boat the *W. J. Behan*. One of the best captains and pilots that worked the Missouri River, Marsh was the man who had brought the wounded from the Battle of the Little Bighorn down to Fort Abraham Lincoln in 1876, traveling the seven hundred miles in fifty-four hours. As the Hunkpapas made their preparations, the officers and their families would have come over to the Hunkpapa camp to say their farewells to the Lakotas they had befriended. During the time that the Hunkpapas had been at Randall, two adult males, six adult females, two male children, and eight female children had died. Of the babies born at Randall, six were males, and ten females. On 28 April, the Lakotas boarded the *Behan*. This time, they went willingly on board, with no signs of sadness or resistance. They were on their way at last.[19]

The boat's load was a heavy one. In addition to the usual freight, there were with the 152 Lakotas, 4 head of beef cattle for their food during the journey, and their military escort of 4 noncommissioned officers and 20 privates of the Fifteenth Infantry, under the command of Lieutenant Thomas F. Davis. Also on board was post surgeon Faulkner as medical officer and Picotte as interpreter. Because the water was low, the journey would be slow. Marsh estimated that it would take about a week to reach Standing Rock. The journey followed the same pattern as their journey down river in 1881, with nightly stops on shore.[20]

The first settlement they tied up at was Chamberlain, where the usual throng of visitors came on board to meet Sitting Bull. Captain Marsh had discovered that, owing to the attentions the chief had received at Fort Randall, he had an "abundant supply of self-esteem and during the northward journey he gave himself the airs of royalty."[21] However, on this particular day, the chief was not in the mood to receive visitors and went below deck to rest. Such was the demand to see him that Marsh had to persuade him to come up and meet his public. Sitting Bull relented, and coming up on deck, smiled regally at the assembled crowd. The usual autograph-signing session followed.

A reporter from the local newspaper, the *Chamberlain Register* conducted the following brief interview:

"Where are you going?"

"Up to Grand River."

"What are you going to do up there?"

"Be a white man and go to farming."

"Are you glad to go to Grand River?"

"Yes."

"Do you understand that you are going onto ground selected for you by the Sioux commission?"

"I own all that land and can go where I please."

"Do you know about the Sioux commission treating with the other Indians and selling some of the land to the government?"

"This is the first time I ever heard of that. I own all the land and nobody can sell it."

"But do you know that the Indians at Pine Ridge and other places have signed an agreement to let the government have the land between the White and Cheyenne Rivers?"

"I don't know that. This is all my land we can see. I was born on it and raised on it and it is mine."

"Don't you know anything about the Sioux commission going to see the Sioux Indians about this land?"

"I know there is three rascally white men going around, but

they can't have my land. This is all my land, I was born and raised on it, and never signed it away. There is lots of thieves all over that will do anything."[22]

The chief would say no more on the subject, and the interview ended. Once again, Sitting Bull made plain his attitude towards the selling of land, a stance that never changed, no matter what pressures were brought to bear on him.

The crowds that had assembled at Chamberlain to see Chief Sitting Bull were so numerous that the military escort had difficulty in controlling them. It was the same on 5 May when the boat docked at Pierre, where the population for miles around came to gaze on the chief and ask for his autograph. The *Saint Paul and Minneapolis Daily Pioneer Press* estimated that he earned two hundred dollars in the trade. During this brief visit, Sitting Bull, wearing a felt hat with a butterfly pinned to it, had his photograph taken by local photographer R. L. Kelley.[23]

The *Behan* left Pierre the following morning and proceeded on its journey up the Missouri towards the Cheyenne River Agency, where Frank Chadron, a half-breed, gave Captain Marsh a fine carved pipestem. Sitting Bull admired the piece, and through his interpreter Picotte, he offered to buy it. The captain did not want to part with it, but Sitting Bull persisted, and Marsh told him, jokingly, that he could have it for fifty dollars. The chief indicated the price was too high. Marsh then told Picotte to tell Sitting Bull that he "had kept me scared for twenty years along the river" and owed him something for that fact alone. With dignity, Sitting Bull replied, "I did not come on your land to scare you. . . . If you had not come on my land, you would not have been scared, either." Nothing more was said, and Marsh kept the pipestem.[24]

The *Behan* continued on its slow journey. At a point about twenty miles below the Standing Rock Agency, the boat passed the first of the Lakota settlements that dotted the reservation. From now on, as the boat progressed towards the agency, groups of Lakotas gathered at intervals on the riverbank to sing songs of greeting to their chief. At 3:00 P.M. on 10 May, the *Behan* finally docked at Fort Yates. A crowd of whites and Lakotas had gathered and were shouting for

130

Sitting Bull, who was sitting in the rear of the pilot house. He eventually appeared, clad in a new blue army overcoat. Sitting Bull had come home to a hero's welcome. However, one newspaper reported that his old lieutenants, Gall and Crow King, "were not effusive in their reception." McLaughlin had made them important men at the agency, and they may have perceived the return of their old leader as a threat to their new status.[25] Or perhaps they simply already knew what Sitting Bull was about to learn.

When the Hunkpapa prisoners of war left Fort Randall, they had numbered 152. During their journey, four men had died, and one baby had been born.[26] Disembarking, they made their camp alongside the Standing Rock Agency, adjacent to Fort Yates, where a newspaper reporter arrived at the chief's tipi to interview him. The reporter described Sitting Bull as looking "ten years younger and twenty fatter than when he surrendered, and though reticent as ever is evidently very glad to return." Asked what he wanted to tell the president and the people, Sitting Bull answered:

> I was a prisoner, but I am not angry or ashamed of that. I am
> glad to be free once more and to return to the place I was born to
> live. I want to die here, and, if unmolested, I will. I want to sleep
> in peace, to plow and sow and raise all I can, I and my people.
> Your people (pointing to the correspondent) do not respect your
> president. You did not respect God, nor his Son, for you killed
> the Son when he came here. I could not expect you to respect
> me and not take my land. . . . But I want to hold the land which
> belongs to me. . . . I want peace. I wish all my enemies could
> come here and be reconciled. The Crows, and even the Red River
> half-breeds, as well as my young men and women, and many
> of the old ones, are scattered far and wide. I wish they could
> be gathered in one place and all could dwell in unity with the
> whites, and that the whites would assist and instruct us to raise
> things from the earth. We were taught to live on buffalo, but I
> am told they are nearly all killed. I would like to have that killing
> stopped if I could. I hear some talk of my going to Grand River to
> farm, thirty-five miles distant. That would suit me very well. My
> heart is pleased.[27]

Agent McLaughlin did not put in an appearance that evening. He remained in his office, where Lieutenant Davis formally handed over his charges into the care of the Indian Department. The agent received a message from Sitting Bull that the chief wanted to meet with him—a request, but with the tone of a demand. McLaughlin's reply, sent across to the Hunkpapa camp the following morning, was equally pointed. He agreed to meet with Sitting Bull, but at "some time in the afternoon when I'm not too busy."[28]

At about three o'clock the next day, Sitting Bull, with an entourage of eighteen to twenty men, arrived at the agency office. The chief was dressed in his blue infantry overcoat, worn over a white shirt and blue cloth leggings. On his feet were porcupine-quill-decorated moccasins, and his hair was braided and wrapped in red cloth. On his head, he wore a slouch hat decorated with several drooping peacock feathers. He must have been disconcerted, if not annoyed, that McLaughlin was not in his office waiting for him. The agent was visiting the agency school. This absence could have been a deliberate ploy on McLaughlin's part to show the chief that he was in charge now. If anybody had to wait, it would be Sitting Bull. The Hunkpapas were ushered into the agency office, where Sitting Bull sat on a chair and the others squatted on the floor.

When McLaughlin eventually appeared, agency interpreter Phillip Wells accompanied him. After the initial greetings, a pipe was lit, passed around, and the agent invited Sitting Bull to speak. If McLaughlin expected a conciliatory speech, he was to be disappointed. The chief began by stating what he expected. He was to be placed first on the agency rolls. He did not want ration tickets issued directly to his people; he would draw the supplies in bulk and distribute them accordingly. He did not intend to take up farming this year, but he would start next year after he had had a chance to see how it was done. McLaughlin recorded these expectations in his annual report for 1883.[29] The *Pioneer Press* reporter, who was also present at this council, gave a more colorful version of the chief's speech:

It is God's will that I should be the chief of all my people. I want to live henceforth at peace with all men, and I desire that all the people belonging to me on this reservation—they are scattered now among many bands—be gathered together so that I may be their chief. It is necessary that this should be so. I cannot keep my young men from doing wrong unless they are where I can control them. If they do wrong, or I do, I want you to tell me about it, and if you do wrong I'll come and tell you. I love and pity my people, and I want you to do the same. When I was a prisoner at Randall I got a letter from the great father (he meant the commissioner of Indian affairs) saying that I was to be freed and sent back here, and that I should have oxen, wagons, and farming impliments given me . . . and I would like to get those things as well as any others that may be due me from the agency stores. I want to wear the same kind of clothes that you do, and to wash them, when soiled, until they wear out. I want . . . to go to Washington, see the great chief, and have a talk with him. I was a prisoner when the commissioners treated with my people for the lands to be taken from the reservation, . . . but I wrote the Great Father and told him I didn't like the way they were acting. In the same letter I told him my objections to the killing of game by the whites. I am a great chief, and I want to be rich. Then I can keep my people straight. Still I can't watch all my Indians any more than the Great Father can watch all his agents. I have here a paper given me by Col. Swaine at Fort Randall (producing it) on which he has written the names of those men whom I want to have made chiefs under me.[30]

At this point, according to the reporter, Sitting Bull laughed heartily as Wells tried to read the names out as they had been written down by a clerk who had his own ideas of spelling. Throughout this speech, which lasted about an hour, McLaughlin listened patiently, gravely uttering an occasional "how," meaning that he understood what was being said, although he would later describe the speech as "inflated nonsense."[31]

Next, it was the major's turn to speak. He began by telling Sitting Bull that he would speak frankly to him, but he would speak honestly. There was nothing in the letter from Washington about Sitting Bull being given oxen, wagons, and farming implements; his people would be given the same share of goods as all the other Lakotas at Standing Rock. The agent explained the efforts he had made in Sitting Bull's behalf while he was in Washington. He went on to say that he would continue to help him all he could; he had already found a good site for Sitting Bull's future camp near the Grand River, which they would both go and look at soon. As to the question of the commissioners, McLaughlin replied that another commission would be at Standing Rock in August. It would consist of powerful men, and what they decided would be right and just. Times had changed; these days "the most industrious man was . . . the biggest chief," and ration tickets would be given to the individual heads of the families in Sitting Bull's band.[32]

The chief responded that he was surprised at the things the major had said. McLaughlin replied that he would always be glad to see him and would help him all he could. Sitting Bull must, however, accept the rules that governed the reservation, just as all the other Lakotas had. The amount of help he would receive depended on how well he adapted to the new way of life. The agent concluded the discussion by saying that it was better to speak the truth now, rather than have the chief believe in things that simply could not be allowed. This final comment ended the first real meeting between the two men who would dominate affairs at Standing Rock for the next seven and a half years.[33]

McLaughlin had been honest and fair in what he told Sitting Bull, and his words were spoken in a firm but gentle manner. He had made the point that the chief was now under his control and appeared confident that Sitting Bull would accept the situation, noting, "Before he left the office he appeared as better satisfied."[34] However, the *Pioneer Press* reporter was probably more accurate regarding Sitting Bull's response to the meeting when he wrote that the chief, "who had entered the council with inflated ideas of his importance, quitted the office with his tail feathers drooping in most salutary fashion."[35] All his demands had been rejected; the only consolation was that he would be going with the major to look at a campsite alongside the Grand River. For the next few months, however, McLaughlin would keep this independent-minded chief near the agency, and not until 1884 would the major fulfill his promise and allow Sitting Bull and his band to move their camp to a new site alongside the Grand River, near where the chief had been born.[36]

Ever since Sitting Bull's surrender, influential white men had courted the chief, anxious to help in his future. Both post commanders, Andrews and Swaine, had proven friendly to their old foe and helpful in dealing with any requests he made as a prisoner of war. At Fort Randall, he had received a steady stream of visitors of importance, both white and Indian. His receptions at the towns he visited on his journeys to and from Fort Randall had been fit for a hero. All indications were that the white man recognized what an important man Sitting Bull was. It was no wonder that he expected such deference to continue. He was a proud man, with the humility among his people that befitted a chief, but his expectations among the white men had outgrown reality.

McLaughlin, as representative of the civilian arm of government, recognized that the Lakotas must alter their lifestyle to survive. They needed to forget the old ways. They must become Christians, take up farming, and have their children educated in schools that would prepare them for the future. Apart from Christianization and the total abandonment of their old culture, Sitting Bull agreed with him that the children needed to learn and change and that his people needed to embrace farming. Although remaining a traditionalist, Sitting Bull would become a district farmer, earning ten dollars a month, and would send his five children to the Grand River Congregational Day School on the reservation to learn the white man's way of life. Initially, McLaughlin may have thought that he and Sitting Bull could work together in the running of the reservation, but Sitting Bull wanted the impossible—he wanted McLaughlin's help in maintaining his chieftainship. In the end, only one man could be in charge, and McLaughlin made sure that it was himself.[37]

EPILOGUE

Sitting Bull was in his early fifties when he arrived at Standing Rock, and, for the most part, he settled down at his home on the Grand River, raising crops and cattle and doting on his children. His health may have been poor, for Congregational missionary Mary Collins reported in 1883 that the chief was "partially paralyzed."[1]

Now that he was no longer a prisoner of war, Sitting Bull did not spend all his time at Standing Rock. He took a number of trips, beginning with a visit to Bismarck in September 1883, shortly after his arrival at the agency. In March 1884, Standing Rock agent James McLaughlin himself took Sitting Bull and One Bull on a two-week trip to Saint Paul, Minnesota, and the chief went to the Minnesota State Fair in September of that year. From June through October 1885, Sitting Bull traveled with Buffalo Bill Cody as part of his Wild West show. As he had throughout his life, and much to McLaughlin's chagrin, Sitting Bull exemplified generosity by spending all the money he made from these and other tours on food and gifts for his followers. In 1886, the chief was one of a hundred Sioux who traveled to the Crow reservation in Montana to feast with his former enemies.[2]

Even though Sitting Bull's ability to move about had increased, his surrender in 1881 had marked the end of the free life of the Lakotas. The vast territory they had once roamed over had been reduced to the confines of the Great Sioux Reservation, and the chief and his followers were the last of the Sioux to accept this situation. Throughout his life, Sitting Bull had fought against white incursion into what he considered to be his land, and now he engaged in a final battle against the government's plans to reduce the size of the reservation.

The chief's first contact with congressional officials came in August 1883, and it was not a success. When Senator Henry L. Dawes held a meeting at Standing Rock as part of an investigation into the actions of the Sioux Land Commission, the chief spoke primarily of his own importance. Ultimately, he was obliged to apologize for his bad behavior.[3] Sitting Bull, however, learned from this mistake. As

negotiations between the tribes and the federal government continued over the next few years, Sitting Bull worked behind the scenes
instead of as a spokesman. He traveled to Washington, D.C., in October 1888 as part of a contingent of Indians who participated in discussions with government representatives. There, the chief took an
active role in private councils but spoke little at public meetings. By
the summer of 1889, however, the government was securing enough
signatures of Lakota men to validate the Sioux Agreement of 1889.
As the men at the Standing Rock Agency waited in line to sign the
agreement, a furious Sitting Bull and twenty of his loyal followers
on horseback charged the waiting Indians, attempting to disrupt the
proceeding. He was unsuccessful, and on 10 February 1890, President
Benjamin Harrison declared that the document had been signed by
the required three-fourths of Indian males. The agreement created
six reservations within western South Dakota and freed more than
nine million acres of land to white settlement.[4] Despite his lifelong
efforts, Sitting Bull had failed to keep the white man out of what
remained of his land.

Following the loss of their territory and their way of life, many Lakotas turned to a new religion in 1889. Paiute Indian Wovoka saw in
a vision a revival of Indian traditions, the return of bountiful game,
and the downfall of the white man. The new religion, the Ghost
Dance, brought hope to the Indians and fear to many white settlers.
Many Lakotas began to dance, particularly on the Pine Ridge and
Rosebud reservations and at Sitting Bull's camp. McLaughlin en-
couraged Sitting Bull to end the dancing, saying it would set back
the gains his people had made and put his followers in danger because the military was being called in to the other agencies. Sitting
Bull refused. Fearing both the dancers and the influence of the chief,
who may have been planning to join the dancers on Pine Ridge reservation, Major General Nelson A. Miles ordered Sitting Bull's arrest.
Early on the morning of 15 December 1890, Indian police came to
the chief's home to take him into custody. A scuffle broke out during which Sitting Bull was shot and killed, along with several others.
The chief was buried in the post cemetery on 17 December. In 1953,
his descendants had Sitting Bull's remains moved to a site near Mo-
bridge, South Dakota.[5]

Although he was obliged to adapt to some of the white man's ways following his surrender in 1881, Sitting Bull remained faithful to his heritage until the end of his life. Despite starvation, imprisonment, and the loss of his land, the chief continued to exemplify the virtues of generosity and courage and to fight for what he thought was best for his people.

ACKNOWLEDGMENTS

The most essential sources for material on Sitting Bull's time at Fort Randall are the Letters Sent, Letters Received, and Post Returns from the National Archives and Records Administration. While the Post Returns are available on microfilm, the Fort Randall Letters Sent and Letters Received are not. I have to thank Trevor K. Plante and the staff of the Textual Archives Service Division, National Archives and Records Administration, for microfilming the Letters Sent for me and for photocopying the Letters Received, all 628 pages. Thank you!

Three newspapers were essential to my research, and all were fortunately available on microfilm. My thanks are due to Steve Neilsen of the Minnesota Historical Society for facilitating my ability to quote extensively from the 4 August 1881 issue of the *Saint Paul and Minneapolis Pioneer Press* containing the interview with Sitting Bull at Fort Yates.

Thanks are due to Khristina L. Stowell and Josh Clough of the University of Oklahoma Libraries for photocopying and guiding me through the material in that treasure trove of western history, the Campbell Collection. At the Smithsonian Institution, I am grateful to Susan McElrath and Jeannie Sklar for guidance with the Alice Fletcher papers and for photocopying Fletcher's Field Diary and handwritten manuscript "Camping with the Sioux" (all 148 pages). Thanks also to Paulette Montileaux at the Journey Museum (Sioux Indian Museum) in Rapid City, South Dakota, for permission to use their photograph of Sitting Bull's medicine bundle and for measuring the cloth it contains to confirm my belief that it was the "flag" waved from the boat as the Lakota prisoners arrived at Fort Yates from Fort Buford.

The state historical societies of Montana, South Dakota, and North Dakota were helpful in supplying photocopies of articles in their out of print publications. Particular thanks go to Ken Stewart at the South Dakota State Historical Society for his advice and encouragement in the early stages of my researches.

For the photographs used, I have to thank the following for their help in identifying what I needed: Sharon Silengo and Mark Halverson (State Historical Society of North Dakota), Chelle Somsen (South Dakota State Historical Society), Terri Raburn (Nebraska State Historical Society), the United States Army Heritage and Education Center at the United States Army Military History Institute, and the staff at both the Prints and Photographs Division, Library of Congress, and the Photographic Archives, Smithsonian Institution.

Thanks to the inventors (whoever they are) of the Internet, the computer, the photocopier, and the microfilm. Without them this book could never have been written. My gratitude also goes to the expert readers who critiqued the manuscript for the South Dakota State Historical Society Press; their advice and guidance improved the final draft. Finally, I wish to thank the editorial staff at the Press for their essential assistance in guiding this book into print.

NOTES

ABBREVIATIONS

The following abbreviations are used in the notes:

AAG   Assistant Adjutant General

AG   Adjutant General

CO   Commanding Officer

CIA   Commissioner of Indian Affairs

NARA National Archives and Records Administration

SW   Secretary of War

SI   Secretary of the Interior

LR   Letters Received

LS   Letters Sent

RG   Record Group

PROLOGUE

1. This background material can be found in many places. For comprehensive treatments, *see especially* George E. Hyde, *Red Cloud's Folk: A History of the Oglala Sioux Indians* (Norman: University of Oklahoma Press, 1975), pp. 3-19, and Raymond J. DeMallie, "The Sioux in Dakota and Montana Territories: Cultural and Historical Background of the Ogden B. Read Collection," in *Vestiges of a Proud Nation: The Ogden B. Read Northern Plains Indian Collection*, ed. Glenn E. Markoe (Burlington, Vt.: Robert Hull Fleming Museum, 1986), pp. 20-21.

2. Robert B. Utley, *The Lance and the Shield: The Life and Times of Sitting Bull* (New York: Henry Holt & Co., 1993), pp. 52-53.

3. Ibid., pp. 67-69, 71-72; Robert G. Athearn, *Forts of the Upper Missouri* (Englewood Cliffs, N.J.: Prentice-Hall, 1967), pp. 123-24, 207. For an overview of the Hunkpapa Lakotas to the time Sitting Bull gained prominence as a tribal leader, *see* Kingsley M. Bray, "Before Sitting Bull: Interpreting Hunkpapa Political History, 1750-1867," *South Dakota History* 40 (Summer 2010): 97-135.

4. Francis Paul Prucha, *American Indian Treaties: The History of a Political Anomaly* (Berkeley: University of California Press, 1994), pp. 282-83; Charles J. Kappler, comp., *Indian Affairs: Laws and Treaties*, Vol.

II: *Treaties* (Washington, D.C.: Government Printing Office, 1904), pp. 998-99; Utley, *Lance and the Shield*, pp. 82-84, 91-92, 115-16.

5. Utley, *Lance and the Shield,* pp. 127, 131-32, 137-44.

6. Ibid., pp. 178-82. For the history of Crazy Horse, *see* Kingsley M. Bray, *Crazy Horse: A Lakota Life*, Civilization of the American Indian Series, vol. 254 (Norman: University of Oklahoma Press, 2006), and Mike Sajna, *Crazy Horse: The Life behind the Legend* (New York: John Wiley & Sons, 2000).

7. For the history of Sitting Bull in Canada, *see* Joseph Manzione, *"I Am Looking to the North for My Life": Sitting Bull, 1876-1881* (Salt Lake City: University of Utah Press, 1991), and Grant MacEwan, *Sitting Bull: The Years in Canada* (Edmonton, Alberta: Hurtig Publishers, 1973).

8. *See* MacEwan, *Sitting Bull*, pp. 124-33.

CHAPTER 1. SURRENDER AT FORT BUFORD

1. The main sources for the surrender at Fort Buford are "Tatonca'o Tocha Talks," *Saint Paul and Minneapolis Daily Pioneer Press* (hereafter *Pioneer Press*), 21 July 1881, and Paul L. Hedren, "Sitting Bull's Surrender at Fort Buford: An Episode in American History," *North Dakota History* 62 (Fall 1995): 2-15. Sources for additional details are given in the notes.

2. Different sources give different numbers, from 183 to 238, for the Lakotas surrendering with Sitting Bull. I have used the numbers (Sitting Bull plus 187 followers) that Major Brotherton recorded in his telegram to General Terry advising him of Sitting Bull's removal from Fort Buford. Brotherton to AAG, Department of Dakota, 29 July 1881, Division of Missouri Special Files, Records of the United States Army Continental Commands, 1821-1920, RG 393, NARA, Microfilm Publication M1495, roll 5, fr. 829. From Fort Buford, Sitting Bull and his followers were transferred to Fort Yates, where their stay (1 August-10 September 1881) coincided with the first reservation-wide census conducted at the Standing Rock Agency. Jerome A. Greene, *Fort Randall on the Missouri, 1856-1892* (Pierre: South Dakota State Historical Society Press, 2005), pp. 139-40. Census takers enumerating members of Sitting Bull's band recorded 195 people living in 41 families. Of these, a number were allowed to stay behind with other family member when the group was transferred to Fort Randall, where they remained incarcerated for the next eighteen months. For the complete listing of Sitting Bull's band and the others recorded in the 1881

Standing Rock census, *see* Ephriam D. Dickson III, *Sitting Bull Surrender Census* (Pierre: South Dakota State Historical Society Press, 2010).

3. Each Lakota tribe was comprised of a number of individual groups known as bands. Each band had its own chief or headman and was made up of relatives and followers of that man. They were loose organizations, with families free to leave and join another band if they disagreed with their leader or wanted to set up a band of their own. The nine bands of the Hunkpapas in the 1880s were the Sore Backs (of horses), Bad Bows, Fresh-Meat-Necklace, Ties-His-Own, Half-a-Breechcloth, Bad-Ones-of-Different-Sorts, *Wakan* ("mysterious"), Legging-Tobacco-Pouch, and the *Tce-oqpa* (translation uncertain but could be obscene). This list appears in James Owen Dorsey, "Siouan Sociology," in *Fifteenth Annual Report of the Bureau of Ethnology to the Secretary of the Smithsonian Institution, 1893-'94* (Washington, D.C.: Government Printing Office, 1897), p. 221. A statement by Swift Dog in Francis Densmore, *Teton Sioux Music* (1918; reprint ed., New York: Da Capo Press, 1972), p. 403, identifies Sitting Bull's band as the Bad Bows.

4. Usher L. Burdick, *Tales from Buffalo Land: The Story of Fort Buford* (Baltimore: Wirth Bros., 1940), pp. 47-48, 89. According to information collected by Burdick, Sitting Bull had two horses, at least, at the time of his surrender. One was possibly a dark bay that was supposedly given to Captain Clifford's wife by the chief soon after his surrender. Sitting Bull then gave the other horse, a small pinto mare about ten years old, to a Major Crompton, the post doctor at Buford, in apparent appreciation for medical treatment. He also allegedly gave the doctor his saddle and a gun; while the first is possible, the second is impossible. There is no record of Sitting Bull being allowed to keep his horses; these individuals may have purchased the animals at an auction held at Buford rather than receiving them personally from the chief.

5. The text of the telegram to Terry and a report of the dispatch to Standing Rock and the reasons for it can be found in "The Story of the Surrender," *Pioneer Press*, 21 July 1881.

6. Robert M. Utley, *The Lance and the Shield: The Life and Times of Sitting Bull* (New York: Henry Holt & Co., 1993), pp. 72-73; Burdick, *Tales from Buffalo Land*, p. 73; Joseph Henry Taylor, *Frontier and Indian Life and Kaleidoscopic Lives* (Valley City, N.Dak.: Washburn's Fiftieth Anniversary Committee, 1932), p. 78.

7. Crazy Horse, with almost nine hundred of his followers, surrendered at Camp Robinson in Nebraska Territory on 6 May 1877. For the first few months, he remained quietly in the vicinity of the agency, but tensions developed between his people and the agency Sioux. Unfounded rumors that he was planning to go back on the warpath prompted the military to arrest him. Troopers brought him into Camp Robinson, allegedly to have a council with the commanding officer, but Crazy Horse quickly realized that he was to be a prisoner not a guest. In an ensuing struggle, the chief was mortally wounded and died about midnight on 5 September 1877. The news of his death spread like wildfire among the Sioux, even to those in Canada, and rumor did not have to exaggerate the event to stiffen the resolve of Sitting Bull never to return across the border. There are many accounts of Crazy Horse's last days. *See* Charles Edmund DeLand, "The Sioux Wars," *South Dakota Historical Collections* 17 (1934): 315-56, and Mike Sajna, *Crazy Horse: The Life behind the Legend* (New York: John Wiley & Sons, 2000), chap. 26.

8. "Tatonca'o Tacha Talks," *Pioneer Press*, 21 July 1881.

9. SW to SI, 27 July, 8 [Aug.] 1881, LS, Records of the Office of the Secretary of War, RG107, NARA, Microfilm Publication M6, roll 82, fr. 246, 257; Bell to SW, 6 Aug. 1881, Indian Division, Records of the Office of the Secretary of the Interior, RG 48, NARA, Microfilm Publication M606, roll 26, fr. 162-63.

10. Brotherton to AAG, 29 July 1881.

CHAPTER 2. JOURNEY TO FORT YATES

1. The principal sources for this chapter are "The Bull Show" and "Piping Times of Peace," *Saint Paul and Minneapolis Pioneer Press* (hereafter *Pioneer Press)*, 1 and 3 Aug. 1881; "Sitting Bull," *Bismarck Tribune*, 5 Aug. 1881; and Stanley Vestal, *New Sources of Indian History, 1850-1891: A Miscellany* (Norman: University of Oklahoma Press, 1934), pp 263-66. The sources for direct quotations or additional material are given in separate notes.

2. Joseph Mills Hanson, *The Conquest of the Missouri: Being the Story of the Life and Exploits of Captain Grant Marsh* (Chicago: A. C. McClurg & Co., 1901), p. 417.

3. Sitting Bull himself stated that Bismarck was the first white town he had seen. "Sitting Bull," *Bismarck Tribune,* 5 Aug. 1881.

4. *See especially* "The Bull Show," *Pioneer Press*, 1 Aug. 1881. The poor

quality of Sitting Bull's clothing is usually attributed to the fact that as chief his role was to be generous towards his people, and consequently, leaders were often not the best-dressed men in camp. Artist Decost Smith, who knew the chief well in later years, said of him, "I have seen him, dressed—as befitted a prominent chief—as poorly as any of his humblest followers" (Smith, *Red Indian Experiences* [London: George Allen & Unwin, 1949], p.185).

5. Usher L. Burdick, *Tales from Buffalo Land: The Story of Fort Buford* (Baltimore: Wirth Bros., 1940), pp. 24-25. *See also* Robert B. Utley, *The Lance and the Shield: The Life and Times of Sitting Bull* (New York: Henry Holt & Co., 1993), p. 237.

6. "Sitting Bull," *Bismarck Tribune*, 5 Aug. 1881.

7. John S. Gray, "The Story of Mrs. Picotte-Galpin, a Sioux Heroine: Eagle Woman Becomes a Trader and Counsels for Peace, 1868-1888," *Montana, the Magazine of Western History* 36 (Summer 1986): 9.

8. "Sitting Bull," *Bismarck Tribune*, 5 Aug. 1881.

9. The last name is a mistranslation and probably refers to The-Bear-That-Looks-Back. The story of this interview appears in "Piping Times of Peace," *Pioneer Press*, 3 Aug. 1881. The number of interpreters present is not clear in the report. It starts off with reference to "the interpreter" but later uses the plural. It was not unusual to have more than one interpreter when dealing with Indians, particularly when accuracy was required.

10. As official interpreter, Allison would have been present and could well have been the instigator of Sitting Bull's refusal to allow an interview without payment, which would have been in keeping with Allison's practice of seeing that Indians got paid for interviews or for having their photographs taken. Allison was not being philanthropic; he would have gotten his share of the fee. Photographer David H. Barry said of Allison: "I took many of my best Indian pictures at Fort Buford in 1880 and 1881. The old Sioux Chiefs demanded money before they would sit. I paid them what they asked (usually a dollar) and several times after I paid them, they would demand more. I could not understand this situation, but finally Gall told me it was Allison who put them up to this work. I hunted up Allison and told him to keep out of my business. . . . I had no more trouble with the chiefs. Allison was well versed in the Sioux language but was unscrupulous, cunning, and altogether bad" (quoted in Burdick, *Tales from Buffalo Land*, p 28).

11. "A Chat with the Chief," *Pioneer Press*, 4 Aug. 1881.

CHAPTER 3. SOJOURN AT STANDING ROCK

1. Robert B. Utley, *The Lance and the Shield: The Life and Times of Sitting Bull* (New York: Henry Holt & Co., 1993), p. 238. The main sources for early events at Fort Yates are "At Fort Yates," "A Chat with the Chief," and "The Bull's New Pasture," *Saint Paul and Minneapolis Pioneer Press* (hereafter *Pioneer Press*), 3, 4, and 7 Aug. 1881, and "Sitting Bull," *Bismarck Tribune*, 5 Aug. 1881. Sources for additional details and direct quotations are given in notes.

2. This cloth and its presentation are described in both "At Fort Yates," *Pioneer Press*, 3 Aug. 1881, and "Sitting Bull," *Bismarck Tribune*, 5 Aug. 1881. Sitting Bull's medicine bag, which contains an object of this description, can be found in the collections of the United States Department of the Interior, Indian Arts and Crafts Board, Sioux Indian Museum, which is housed within the Journey Museum in Rapid City, S.Dak. For more on medicine bags and war charms, *see* James R. Walker, *Lakota Belief and Ritual*, ed. Raymond J. DeMallie and Elaine A. Jahner (Lincoln: University of Nebraska Press, 1980), esp. pp. 264-66.

3. *Pioneer Press*, 3 Aug. 1881, says "my love." *Bismarck Tribune*, 5 Aug., says "my son."

4. Sitting Bull tells of her visit in "A Chat with the Chief," *Pioneer Press*, 4 Aug. 1881. The name of Many Horses' first husband is not known. Whoever he was, her father disapproved of him and had rejected the usual gifts brought to him for his daughter's hand in marriage. While he was away, the couple had eloped, not an unusual occurrence in Lakota life. Eloping couples would eventually return to their camp where they would be accepted as man and wife, it being considered too late to do anything about it. Utley, *Lance and the Shield*, pp. 226, 240.

5. The list of guests can be found in "A Chat with the Chief," *Pioneer Press*, 4 Aug. 1881. I have been unable to find out who Chief Rauber was; he was not an Indian. I have also corrected the rank of Captain George M. Downey. In the original newspaper report, he is listed as lieutenant, but according to Francis B. Heitman's *Historical Register and Dictionary of the United States Army, from Its Organization, September 29, 1789, to March 2, 1903*, 2 vols. (Washington D.C.: Government Printing Office, 1903), 1:381, there is only one Downey that fits in that period of time.

6. This quotation and all that follow from this interview can be found in "A Chat with the Chief," *Pioneer Press*, 4 Aug. 1881.

146

7. Garfield, who had been shot on 2 July, would not die until 19 September 1881.

8. Mathew Stirling, *Three Pictographic Autobiographies of Sitting Bull*, Smithsonian Miscellaneous Collections, vol. 97, no. 5 (Washington, D.C.: Smithsonian Institution, 1938), pp. 3-34; John Williamson to Andrews, 12 Dec. 1881, Fort Randall LR, Records of the United States Army Continental Commands, 1821-1920, RG 393, NARA, Washington, D.C. Of the three records in the Smithsonian publication, only the one recorded by James Kimball, a military surgeon, contains encounters with white men. Lakotas familiar with Sitting Bull's war record gave the portrayal of events to Kimball. Sitting Bull more or less approved of the account when he was shown the drawings in December 1881, which is discussed in Chapter 6 ahead. In the scale of Lakota war honors, the killing of an enemy ranks below the act of counting coup, making his record of fifteen coups against white men an indication of his prowess as a warrior.

9. "The Bull's New Pasture," *Pioneer Press*, 7 Aug. 1881; "News from Sitting Bull," *Bismarck Tribune*, 26 Aug. 1881.

10. "The Bull's New Pasture," *Pioneer Press*, 7 Aug. 1881. The *tiyotipi* was a larger than normal tipi where the chiefs and headmen met and governed their camp. It also served as a community center for important feasts and ceremonies.

11. Ibid.

12. Ibid.

13. For an account of this remarkable woman, *see* John S. Gray's two-part essay, "The Story of Mrs. Picotte-Galpin," *Montana, the Magazine of Western History* 36 (Spring 1986): 2-21 and (Summer 1986): 2-21.

14. "Affairs at Standing Rock," *Pioneer Press*, 15 Aug. 1881; Louis L. Pfaller, *James McLaughlin: The Man with an Indian Heart* (New York: Vantage Press, 1978), pp. 59-60; "Savage Sioux," *Bismarck Tribune*, 26 Aug. 1881.

15. "News from Sitting Bull," *Bismarck Tribune*, 26 Aug. 1881; "The Bending Bovine," *Pioneer Press*, 1 Sept. 1881.

16. "The Bending Bovine," *Pioneer Press*, 1 Sept. 1881. For more on the Northern Cheyennes, *see* Stan Hoig, *Perilous Pursuit: The U.S. Cavalry and the Northern Cheyennes* (Boulder: University Press of Colorado, 2002).

17. "Aboriginal Assurance" and "Hostile Sioux," *Pioneer Press*, 2 and 4 Sept. 1881.

CHAPTER 4. REMOVAL TO FORT RANDALL

1. "They Had to Bind Bull," *Saint Paul and Minneapolis Pioneer Press* (hereafter *Pioneer Press*), 12 Sept. 1881.

2. Quoted in "Affairs at Standing Rock," ibid., 15 Aug. 1881.

3. Drum to Sheridan, Washington, D.C., [22] Aug. 1881, Division of Missouri Special Files, Records of the United States Army Continental Commands, 1821-1920, RG 393, NARA, Microfilm Publication M1495, roll 5, fr. 842.

4. Editorial, *Bismarck Tribune*, 2 Sept. 1881.

5. Quoted in Louis L. Pfaller, *James McLaughlin: The Man with an Indian Heart* (New York: Vantage Press, 1978), p. 93.

6. AAG, Department of Dakota, to CO, Fort Yates, 1 Sept. 1881, M1495, roll 5, fr. 852.

7. Gilbert to AAG, Department of Dakota, 2 Sept. 1881, ibid., fr. 855.

8. "By Telegraph: Sitting Bull, Disgusted and Defiant," *Bismarck Tribune*, 9 Sept. 1881.

9. Quoted in *Sitting Bull: The Years in Canada*, by Grant MacEwan (Edmonton, Alberta: Hurtig Publishers, 1973), p. 128.

10. For more on the Minnesota Uprising and the fate of the Santee prisoners, see Kenneth Carley, *The Dakota War of 1862: Minnesota's Other Civil War* (Saint Paul: Minnesota Historical Society Press, 1976), and Gary Clayton Anderson, *Little Crow: Spokesman for the Sioux* (Saint Paul: Minnesota Historical Society Press, 1986).

11. My main sources for the removal of Sitting Bull's band from Fort Yates are "The Angry Bull" and "They Had to Bind Bull," *Pioneer Press*, 11 and 12 Sept. 1881. Sources for additional details are given where appropriate.

12. "Sitting Bull Satisfied," ibid., 8 Sept. 1881.

13. The incident is reported in "The Angry Bull," ibid., 11 Sept. 1881. It is also recorded in Sally Roesch Wagner, ed., *Daughters of Dakota, Volume II: Stories from the Attic* (Yankton, S.Dak.: By the Editor, 1990), p. 21.

14. The woman was probably Mrs. Crazy Dog, see ahead, Chapter 5.

15. "They Had to Bind Bull," *Pioneer Press*, 12 Sept. 1881, based on a telegram from Pierre, D.T., claimed that the soldiers bound the chief and carried him on board, but an earlier report from Fort Yates, "The Angry Bull," ibid., 12 Sept., contained no such detail.

148   16. James McLaughlin, *My Friend the Indian* (1910; reprint ed., Lin-

coln: University of Nebraska Press, 1989), pp. 182-83. For McLaughlin's assessment of their relationship, *see* pp. 34-35.

17. "Among the Sioux," *Yankton Daily Press and Dakotaian*, 28 Oct. 1881.

18. The fact of a child being born into Sitting Bull's family on the boat can be inferred from the lists of Indian prisoners of war (*see* Jerome A. Greene, *Fort Randall on the Missouri, 1856-1892* [Pierre: South Dakota State Historical Press, 2005], app. C), which recorded a female infant, one day old. There is no documentation as to who the mother was, but I have assumed it was Four Robes because, in the photographs taken of the family at Fort Randall, it is the younger wife who is holding the young child.

19. Greene, *Fort Randall*, pp. 108-9, 113-24.

20. Andrews to AAG, Department of Dakota, 3 Jan. 1882, Fort Randall LS, 2 Jan. 1882-19 July 1883, no 5, RG 393, NARA, Washington, D.C.; Post Returns, Fort Randall, Sept. 1881, Records of the Adjutant General's Office, 1780s-1917, RG 94, NARA, Microfilm Publication M617, roll 990. There are two surviving lists of the Lakotas who were turned over to Colonel Andrews: (A) "List of Indians (Sitting Bull Party) Turned over at Fort Randall, DT," 11 Sept. 1881, compiled by Captain Henry Howe, Fort Yates LR, 13 June 1883, no. 593, RG393, NARA. This same list can also be found in the James McLaughlin Papers, Assumption College Archives, Richardton, N.Dak., microfilm ed., roll 31. (B) "List of Indian Prisoners of War (Sitting Bull's Band) turned over by Captain H. S. Howe, 17th Infantry, to Colonel G. L. Andrews, 25th Infantry, on the 18th day of September 1881," Fort Randall LR (there is one page missing from this list). Comparison between the two lists is confusing, but for handy reference, Greene provides a compilation as Appendix C in his *Fort Randall*, pp. 185-91, although he counts 172 prisoners, including Shoot-the-Bear and family, who were probably omitted from the prisoner count in the Post Returns, which was used as the tally for morning roll calls. Both lists appear to have been written out and/or amended at a later date than the prisoner handover at Fort Randall on 18 September 1881. List A is probably the earliest and, given its date of 11 September, may have originated as a list of the prisoners onboard the stern-wheeler from Yates. Shoot-the-Bear is shown with the note "returned to Standing Rock Agency on the *Sherman*," which occurred on the day of the handover, and Mrs. Crazy Horse's (Dog's) husband is not mentioned. On List B, against the name of Mrs. Crazy Horse (Dog), is the note, "Man absent joined at Fort Randall afterwards," which

happened in October 1881. To confuse things completely, list B records Brave Bear, wife and child, but it could be read as Brave Bear's wife and child. Brave Bear left Sitting Bull's band at Fort Yates.

21. Andrews to AG, Department of Dakota, 19 Sept. 1881, Fort Randall LS, 1 July 1880-30 Dec. 1881, no 169.

22. My placement of Sitting Bull's family members in the two tipis is conjecture. As the average number of inhabitants of a tipi was six adults, I have assumed that his teenage daughters lived in the second tipi with his mother. Sitting Bull would have preferred to have his immediate family with him in his own tipi, and such might have been the case; after all, there were fourteen people in his tipi when he was interviewed by the *Pioneer Press* reporter at Fort Yates. His stepsons, Little Soldier and Blue Turtle, were later known, respectively, as Louis and John (or William) Sitting Bull. The latter was a deaf mute.

23. Greene, *Fort Randall*, p. 140.

24. Ibid., pp. 126, 144, 224n2; W. Boyes, *Custer's Black White Man* (Washington, D.C.: Walbenjon Associates, 1972); John H. Nankivell, *Buffalo Soldier Regiment: History of the Twenty-fifth United States Infantry, 1869-1926*, Bison Books ed. (Lincoln: University of Nebraska Press, 2001), p. 36.

25. Andrews to AG, Department of Dakota, 19 Sept. 1881.

26. George P. Ahern to Captain W. S. Campbell, 12 and 31 July 1929, Box 107, Walter Stanley Campbell Collection, Western History Collections, University of Oklahoma Libraries, Norman; Alice Cunningham Fletcher, "Camping with the Sioux: Fieldwork Diary," 27-29 Oct. 1881, National Anthropological Archives, Smithsonian Institution, www.nmnh.si.edu/naa/fletcher. Fletcher noted, "When Sitting Bull's camp is counted, the women and children form a ring in the center of the enclosure, the men sitting by the tent door"—a variation that could have been caused by alterations in roll-call procedure; her account is for 1881, and Ahern's is for 1882. She mentioned that Sitting Bull stayed in his "tent," which would not have been normal practice, but it is possible that his eyes were troubling him again on that occasion.

27. Carole Barrett, "One Bull: A Man of Good Understanding," *North Dakota History* 66 (Summer/Fall 1999): 4; "Piping Times of Peace," *Pioneer Press*, 3 Aug. 1881. Luther Standing Bear says it was a common practice for Lakotas to salute the sun in the morning. *See* his *Land of the Spotted Eagle* (Boston: Houghton Mifflin Co., 1933), p. 47.

28. For information on games, *see* Royal B. Hassrick, *The Sioux: Life and Customs of a Warrior Society* (Norman: University of Oklahoma Press, 1964), pp. 127-34, and Luther Standing Bear, *My People the Sioux* (Boston: Houghton Mifflin Co., 1928), pp. 28-48.

29. Hassrick, *The Sioux,* pp. 133-34; Standing Bear, *My People the Sioux,* pp. 35-37.

30. Hassrick, *The Sioux*, pp. 140-43.

31. For the role of the *akicita*, *see* James R. Walker, *Lakota Society*, ed. Raymond J. DeMallie (Lincoln: University of Nebraska Press, 1982), pp. 28-29.

32. Ahern to Campbell, 12 July 1929.

33. The details and schedules of army routine at frontier forts can be found in Don Rickey, Jr., *Forty Miles a Day on Beans and Hay: The Enlisted Soldier Fighting the Indian Wars* (Norman: University of Oklahoma Press, 1963), chap. 6, and Greene, *Fort Randall*, p. 135.

34. Post Trader to SW, 18, 20 Nov. 1882, Fort Randall LS, 2 Jan. 1882-29 July 1883, no. 208; Greene, *Fort Randall*, p. 108.

35. William John Armstrong, "Sitting Bull and a Michigan Family: Legacy of an Unlikely Friendship," *Michigan History* 79 (Jan.-Feb. 1995): 28-34.

36. Andrews to AAG, Department of Dakota, 26 Sept. 1881, Fort Randall LS, 1 July 1880-30 Dec. 1881, no. 177.

37. Sheridan to AG of the Army, Chicago, 27 Apr. 1881, M1495, roll 5, fr. 725.

CHAPTER 5. FORT RANDALL, SEPTEMBER-NOVEMBER 1881

1. Post Adjutant to Yankton Agent, 23 Sept. 1881, Fort Randall LS, 1 July 1880-30 Dec. 1881, no. 176, Records of the United States Army Continental Commands, 1821-1920, RG 393, NARA, Washington, D.C.

2. Yankton Agent to Andrews, 23 Sept. 1881, Fort Randall LR, no. 382, ibid.

3. Ibid., 28 Sept. 1881, no. 391; Andrews to Indian Agent, Yankton Agency, 30 Sept. 1881, Fort Randall LS, no. 181.

4. Walking Elk to Andrews, 3 Dec. 1881, Fort Randall LR, no #.

5. At the end of the list of prisoners of war compiled by Captain Howes (*see* Jerome A. Greene, *Fort Randall on the Missouri, 1856-1892* [Pierre: South Dakota State Historical Press, 2005], p. 191) is a lone woman named Mrs. Crazy Horse, a mistranslation of her husband's name. No listing of

151

a Crazy Horse occurs in the censuses of Hunkpapas at Standing Rock. The nearest name to it is Crazy Dog. Indian Census Rolls, 1884-1940, Records of the Bureau of Indian Affairs, RG 75, NARA, Microfilm Publication M595, roll 547, fr. 108. For a full listing, *see* Ephriam Dickson III, *Sitting Bull Surrender Census* (Pierre: South Dakota State Historical Society Press, 2010).

6. For accounts of Lakotas visiting white settlers, *see* Sally Roesch Wagner, ed., *Daughters of Dakota, Vol. III: Stories of Friendship between the Settlers and the Dakota Indians* (Yankton, S.Dak.: By the Editor, 1990).

7. Andrews to AG, Department of Dakota, and CO, Fort Yates, 12 Oct. 1881, Fort Randall LS, nos. 191, 192.

8. AAG, Department of Dakota, to CO, Fort Randall, 17 Oct. 1881, Fort Randall LR, no. 433.

9. Paul Boyton, *The Story of Paul Boyton: A Rare Tale of Travel and Adventure* (London: George Routledge & Sons, 1893), pp. 326-29. For a description of Boyton's rubber suit, *see* pp. 105-6

10. James Creelman, *On the Great Highway: The Wanderings and Adventures of a Special Correspondent* (Boston: Lothrop Publishing Co., 1901), pp. 297-303. The act of putting the thumbs together that Creelman noted could be sign language. The word "together" is the same sign as "with," which is made by placing the thumbs together but with the fingers extended. *See* W. P. Clark, *The Indian Sign Language, with Brief Explanatory Notes, . . . Signals of Our Aborigines* (Philadelphia: L. R. Hamersly & Co., 1885), pp. 380, 407.

11. Creelman, *On the Great Highway,* p. 303.

12. Rudolf Cronau, "My Visit among the Hostile Dakota Indians and How They Became My Friends," *South Dakota Historical Collections* 22 (1946): 413, 416.

13. Ibid., pp. 417-18.

14. Francis Paul Prucha, *American Indian Policy in Crisis: Christian Reformers and the Indian, 1865-1900* (Norman: University of Oklahoma Press, 1976), p. 114-15; Joan Mark, *A Stranger in Her Native Land: Alice Fletcher and the American Indian* (Lincoln: University of Nebraska Press, 1988), pp. 59-60. For more on *Standing Bear* v. *Crook, see* Valerie Sherer Mathes and Richard Lowitt, *The Standing Bear Controversy: Prelude to Indian Reform* (Urbana: University of Illinois Press, 2003).

15. How Sitting Bull managed a messenger is unknown; he could not

have sent a runner from his own camp, for it would not have been allowed, and no absentees are indicated in the Fort Randall post returns.

16. The details of Tibbles and Fletcher's visit to Fort Randall presented in this chapter are taken from Thomas Henry Tibbles, *Buckskin and Blanket Days: Memoirs of a Friend of the Indians* (New York: Doubleday & Co., 1957), pp. 289-93, and Alice Cunningham Fletcher, Field Diary, n.p., MS 4558, Series 9, Alice Fletcher and Frances La Flesche Papers, National Anthropological Archives, Smithsonian Institution, Washington, D.C. *See also* Mark, *A Stranger in Her Native Land*, pp. 58, 60-63, and Alice Cunningham Fletcher, "Camping with the Sioux: Fieldwork Diary," 25-29 Oct. 1881, National Anthropological Archives, Smithsonian Institution, www.nmnh.si.edu/naa/fletcher.

17. Tibbles, *Buckskin and Blanket Days*, p. 291.

18. Fletcher, Field Diary, n.p.

19. Fletcher, "Camping with the Sioux: Fieldwork Diary," 27-29 Oct. 1881; Tibbles, *Buckskin and Blanket Days*, pp. 291-92; Breck to CO, Fort Randall, 3 Nov. 1881, Fort Randall LR, no #.

20. Fletcher, "Camping with the Sioux: Fieldwork Diary," 27-29 Oct. 1881. *See also* Mark, *Stranger in Her Native Land*, p. 61.

21. Fletcher, "Camping with the Sioux: Fieldwork Diary," 27-29 Oct. 1881. The specific details of erecting and dismantling a Lakota tipi can be found in Fletcher's handwritten "Camping with the Sioux," MS 4558, Series 5, pp. 105, 108, Fletcher and LaFlesche Papers. Both this handwritten manuscript and the typewritten version that appears on the Smithsonian Institution website were based on Fletcher's field diaries of her visits with the Lakotas in 1881 and 1882.

22. Fletcher, Field Diary, n.p.

23. Ibid.

24. Mark, *Stranger in Her Native Land*, p. 62.

25. Cronau, "My Visit among the Hostile Dakota Indians," pp. 417, 419. For Sitting Bull's pictographs, *see* Mathew Stirling, *Three Pictographic Autobiographies of Sitting Bull*, Smithsonian Miscellaneous Collections, vol. 97, no. 5 (Washington, D.C.: Smithsonian Institution, 1938).

26. Cronau, "My Visit among the Hostile Dakota Indians," pp. 419-20.

CHAPTER 6. FORT RANDALL, NOVEMBER-DECEMBER 1881

1. Marty traveled to Canada with permission from the War Department, but he did not have authority to negotiate deals. Although Marty,

his interpreter, a scout, and a small escort of agency Lakotas were cordially received and spent several days in council with the hostile chiefs, the abbot was not successful in negotiating a surrender. For an account of Marty's peace mission, *see* J. B. A. Brouillet, "Abbot Martin Visits Sitting Bull," *Annals of the Catholic Indian Missions* 2 (Jan. 1878): 7-10, and Robert F. Karolevitz, *Bishop Martin Marty: "The Black Robe Lean Chief"* (Yankton, S.Dak.: By the Author, 1980), pp. 66-68. For the efforts of another missionary, *see* Louis L. Pfaller, "The Galpin Journal: Dramatic Record of an Odyssey of Peace," *Montana, the Magazine of Western History* 18 (Apr. 1968): 2-23.

2. News item, *Yankton Daily Press and Dakotaian*, 15 Nov. 1881.

3. Marty to Andrews, Nov. 1881, Fort Randall LR, no. 455, Records of the United States Army Continental Commands, 1821-1920, RG 393, NARA, Washington, D.C.

4. Andrews to Marty, 11 Nov. 1881, Fort Randall LS, no. 206, ibid.

5. SW to Williamson, 12 Nov. 1881, SW, LS, Records of the Office of the Secretary of War, RG 107, NARA, Microfilm Publication M6, roll 83, fr. 51.

6. Hare to Andrews, 5 Nov. 1881, Fort Randall LR, no. 452.

7. Andrews to AAG, Department of Dakota, 30 Nov. 1881, and Andrews to CO, Fort Yates, 13 Dec. 1881, Fort Randall LS, nos. 213, 222. Many-Old-Men appeared in the prisoner count for November 1881, according to the post return, but was not among the count for December 1881. Post Returns, Fort Randall, Sept., Nov., Dec. 1881, Jan. 1882, Records of the Adjutant General's Office, 1780s-1917, RG 94, NARA, Microfilm Publication M617, roll 990.

8. Andrews to AAG, Department of Dakota, 3 Jan. 1882, Fort Randall LS, no. 5.

9. For a discussion of winter on the Northern Great Plains, *see* Everett Dick, *The Sod House Frontier* (New York: D. Appleton-Century Co., 1937), pp. 221-30.

10. Post Returns, Fort Randall, Dec. 1881.

11. Williamson to Andrews, 12 Dec. 1881, Fort Randall LR, no #; Mathew Stirling, *Three Pictographic Autobiographies of Sitting Bull*, Smithsonian Miscellaneous Collections, vol. 97, no. 5 (Washington, D.C.: Smithsonian Institution, 1938), pp. 3-7.

12. Williamson to Andrews, 12 Dec. 1881.

13. Details concerning the handling of the pictographic war record are

found in Andrews to CO, Fort Yates, 30 Nov. 1881, no. 212, Andrews to AAG, Department of Dakota, 14 Dec. 1881, no. 225, and Endorsements, 30 Dec. 1881, 7 Jan. 1882, all in Fort Randall LS.

14. Williamson to Andrews, 12 Dec. 1881, Fort Randall LR, no #. This letter is different from the one referred to in note 13. There are two unnumbered copies of letters sent on the same date.

15. Ibid.

16. Luther Standing Bear, *My People the Sioux* (New York: Houghton Mifflin Co., 1928), p.185; Robert M. Utley, *The Lance and the Shield: The Life and Times of Sitting Bull* (New York: Henry Holt & Co., 1993), pp. 262-64; George P. Ahern to W. S. Campbell, 31 July 1929, Box 107, Walter Stanley Campbell Collection, Western History Collections, University of Oklahoma Libraries, Norman. For a summary of the fights at Cedar Creek and Ash Creek, *see* Utley, *Lance and the Shield*, pp. 170-72, 178-79.

17. For more on punishment of criminals within Indian society, *see* Robert H. Lowie, *Indians of the Plains* (Garden City, N.Y.: Natural History Press, 1963), pp. 125-26, and Paul N. Carlson, *The Plains Indians*, Elma Dill Russell Spencer Series in the West and Southwest, no. 19 (College Station: Texas A & M University Press, 1998), p. 75.

18. Andrews to AAG, Department of Dakota, 6 Jan. 1882, Fort Randall LS, no. 10. *See also* Jerome A. Greene, *Fort Randall on the Missouri, 1856-1892* (Pierre: South Dakota State Historical Society Press, 2005), p. 144. For another perspective on Andrews's decision to dismiss the alleged rapists from the military, *see* Betti VanEpps-Taylor, *Forgotten Lives: African Americans in South Dakota* (Pierre: South Dakota State Historical Society Press, 2008), p. 45.

19. Quoted in Robert M. Utley, *Frontier Regulars: The United States Army and the Indian, 1866-1891* (New York: Macmillan Publishing Co., 1973), p. 26. For a brief assessment of the African American regiments, *see* ibid., pp. 25-28.

20. Greene, *Fort Randall on the Missouri*, pp. 144, 231n37.

CHAPTER 7. FORT RANDALL, JANUARY-APRIL 1882

1. Andrews to Hare, 23 Dec. 1881, Fort Randall LS, 1 July 1880-30 Dec. 1881, no. 231, Records of the United States Army Continental Commands, 1821-1920, RG 393, NARA, Washington, D.C.

2. Hare to Andrews, Niobrara Mission, 28 Dec. 1881, Fort Randall LR, no #, ibid.

3. Andrews to Hare, 30 Dec. 1881, Fort Randall LS, no. 237.

4. Endorsement, 5 Jan. 1882, Fort Randall LS, no. 11.

5. M. A. DeWolfe Howe, *The Life and Labors of Bishop Hare: Apostle to the Sioux* (New York: Sturgis & Walton Co., 1914), p. 63.

6. Hare to Mary A. Emery, 5 Jan. 1874, quoted ibid., pp. 97-98.

7. Quoted ibid, p. 97. For more on the Carlisle and Hampton boarding schools, *see* David Wallace Adams, *Education for Extinction: American Indians and the Boarding School Experience, 1875-1928* (Lawrence: University of Kansas, 1995), and Donal F. Lindsey, *Indians at Hampton Institute, 1877-1923* (Urbana: University of Illinois Press, 1995).

8. Howe, *Life and Labors of Bishop Hare*, p. 53.

9. Endorsement, 5 Jan. 1882, Fort Randall LS, no. 11.

10. Andrews to AAG, Department of Dakota, 28 Sept. 1881, Fort Randall LR, no. 179.

11. Andrews to AAG, Department of Dakota, 17 Jan. 1882, Fort Randall LS, no. 18.

12. AAG, Department of Dakota, to Andrews, 3 Dec. 1881, 13 Jan. (telegram), and copy of telegram, AAG, Military Division of the Missouri, to Terry, 23 Jan. 1882, all in Fort Randall LR, no #s; Andrews to AAG, Department of Dakota, 3, 17, 21 Jan. 1882, Fort Randall LS, nos. 6, 18, and 23.

13. Chief Clerk, War Department, to Governor of Michigan, 14 Sept. 1881, and SW to President pro tem of the United States Senate, 28 Feb. 1882, both SW, LS, 1800-1889, Records of the Office of the Secretary of War, RG 107, NARA, Microfilm Publication M6, roll 83, fr. 104, and roll 84, fr. 391; SI to CIA, 12 Aug. 1881, Indian Division, Records of the Office of the Secretary of the Interior, RG 48, NARA, Microfilm Publication 606, roll 27, fr. 69.

14. SW to SI, 17 Feb. 1882, SW, LS, M6, roll 84, fr. 88.

15. Depot Quartermaster to Andrews, 18 Mar., 11 Sept. 1882, Fort Randall LR, nos. 143, 473; Andrews to Depot Quartermaster, 22 Mar., 14 Sept. 1882, Fort Randall LS, nos. 60, 162.

16. For evidence of these epidemics in winter counts, *see* James H. Howard, "Dakota Winter Counts as a Source of Plains History," in *Anthropological Papers, Numbers 57-62*, Smithsonian Institution, Bureau of American Ethnology, Bulletin no. 173 (Washington, D.C.: Government Printing Office, 1960), pp. 374, 377-78. For a dramatic account of the 1837 smallpox epidemic, *see* R. G. Robertson, *Rotting Face: Smallpox and the American Indian* (Caldwell, Idaho: Caxton Press, 2001).

17. "The Transfer of Sitting Bull," *Saint Paul and Minneapolis Pioneer Press* (hereafter *Pioneer Press*), 29 Mar. 1882.

18. Ibid.

19. News item, *Yankton Daily Press and Dakotaian*, 5 Apr. 1882.

20. Post Returns, Fort Randall, Mar. 1882, Records of the Adjutant General's Office, 1780s-1917, RG 94, NARA, Microfilm Publication M617, roll 990.

21. Andrews to agents at Standing Rock, Lower Brulé, and Rosebud, 21 Mar. 1882, Fort Randall LS, nos. 55, 56, 57.

22. Parkhurst to Andrews, 30 Mar. 1882, no. 197, and McLaughlin to Andrews, 7 Apr. 1882, no. 215, Fort Randall LR, no #s.

23. McLaughlin to Andrews, 5 July 1882, Fort Randall LR, no #; Andrews to McLaughlin, 19 July 1882, Fort Randall LS, no. 116. Scared Bear was in poor health, partially paralyzed, and unable to travel, McLaughlin reported, adding that the old man wanted to stay at Standing Rock and wanted his wife, still at Fort Randall, to join him. McLaughlin told Andrews that if the Hunkpapa's health improved he would send him back to the fort, but Scared Bear was still at Standing Rock in September 1882; it is probable that he was not reunited with his wife until Sitting Bull's band returned to that agency. McLaughlin to Andrews, 27 July 1882, Fort Randall LR, no #; Lawson to McLaughlin, Fort Randall, 25 Sept. 1882, Fort Randall LS, no. 171.

24. This photograph can be found in Library and Archives Canada, negative no. C19024, Ottawa, Ontario, Canada. It is reproduced in Joseph Manzione, *"I Am Looking to the North for My Life": Sitting Bull 1876-1881* (Salt Lake City: University of Utah Press, 1991), p. 92.

25. Details of the photographic process come from Wesley R. Hurt and William E. Lass, *Frontier Photographer: Stanley J. Morrow's Dakota Years* (Lincoln: University of Nebraska Press, 1956), pp. 45-51.

26. The photograph "Stealing the Trade," produced in 1882 by Bailey, Dix, and Mead, is sometimes said to be of the photographer, but the man is wearing leggings and moccasins and looks a little like Sitting Bull himself. The image can be found in Jerome A. Greene, *Fort Randall on the Missouri, 1856-1892* (Pierre: South Dakota State Historical Society Press, 2005), p. 157.

27. All twenty-four photographs are reproduced in Greene, *Fort Randall on the Missouri, 1865-1892*, pp. 149-64, which suggests that Morrow is the photographer. *See also* Frank Goodyear, "The Narratives of Sit-

ting Bull's Surrender: Bailey, Dix, and Mead's Photographic Western," in *Dressing in Feathers: The Construction of the Indian in American Popular Culture*, ed. S. Elizabeth Bird (Boulder, Colo.: Westview Press, 1996), pp. 30, 42nn12, 13, 16, which identifies the photographer as Cross.

28. Winifred W. Barton, *John P. Williamson: A Brother to the Sioux* (New York: Fleming H. Revell Co., 1919), p.167.

29. Williamson to Andrews, 25 Apr. 1882; and Bentzoni to Officer of the Day, 29 Apr. 1882, both Fort Randall LR.

CHAPTER 8. FORT RANDALL, MAY–AUGUST 1882

1. Post Returns, Fort Randall, Apr., May 1882, Records of the Adjutant General's Office, 1780s-1917, RG 94, NARA, Microfilm Publication M617, roll 990.

2. Post Adjutant to Post Surgeon, 20 May 1882, Fort Randall LS, 2 January 1882-29 July 1883, no. 87, Records of the United States Army Continental Commands, 1821-1920, RG 393, NARA, Washington, D.C.

3. George P. Ahern to Capt. W. S. Campbell, 31 July 1929, Box 107, Walter Stanley Campbell Collection, Western History Collections, University of Oklahoma Libraries, Norman; Royal B. Hassrick, *The Sioux: Life and Customs of a Warrior Society* (Norman: University of Oklahoma Press, 1964), p. 295.

4. George E. Hyde, *A Sioux Chronicle* (Norman: University of Oklahoma Press, 1956), p. 75. There are many accounts of the Sioux Sun Dance, all of which have minor variations due to the individual beliefs of the shaman in charge. Two of the best eyewitness accounts can be found in J. R. Walker, "The Sun Dance and Other Ceremonies of the Ogalala Division of the Teton Dakota," *American Museum of Natural History Anthropological Papers* 16 (1917): 60-120, and Alice C. Fletcher, "Sun Dance of the Ogallala Sioux," *Proceedings of the American Association for the Advancement of Science* 30 (1883): 580-84. For the revival of the Sun Dance, *see* Ethel Nurge, ed., *The Modern Sioux: Social Systems and Reservation Culture* (Lincoln: University of Nebraska Press, 1970), p. 287.

5. Andrews to AAG, Department of Dakota, 28 June 1882, Fort Randall LS, no. 99.

6. Petition, residents of Sunnyside Holt County, Neb., to Andrews, 24 June 1882, and Petition, residents of Kaya Coha, Neb., to Andrews, 26 June 1882, both Fort Randall LR, no #s, RG 393; Andrews to AAG, Department of Dakota, 28 June 1882, Fort Randall LS, no. 99.

7. Bentzoni to Post Adjutant, 17 July 1882, Fort Randall LR, no. 367.

8. James McLaughlin, *My Friend the Indian* (1910; reprint ed., Lincoln: University of Nebraska Press, 1989), pp. 30-32.

9. For accounts of this buffalo hunt, *see* Francie M. Berg, *The Last Great Buffalo Hunts* (Hettinger, N.Dak.: Dakota Buttes Visitors Council, 1995), pp. 5, 9-20; McLaughlin, *My Friend the Indian*, pp. 97-116.

10. J. B. Hassert to Martin Marty, 14 June 1882, Bureau of Catholic Indian Missions Records (hereafter BCIMR), Marquette University Libraries, microfilm ed., roll 5, fr. 390.

11. Andrews to AAG, Department of Dakota, 4 July 1882, Fort Randall LS, no. 104.

12. Ibid. In this letter, Andrews refers to White Dog as White Swan, an error he corrected in subsequent letters. According to the prisoner of war lists, White Dog had two daughters: twenty-three-year-old The-Lodge-Beyond and seventeen-year-old Eagle-Wing-Woman. Jerome A. Greene, *Fort Randall on the Missouri, 1856-1892* (Pierre: South Dakota State Historical Society Press, 2005), pp. 185-86.

13. Crow Dog was convicted of the murder of Spotted Tail in March 1882, and after appeals, would be released in December 1883. Brave Bear, Sitting Bull's son-in-law, was found guilty of killing Joseph Johnson, a white man, in January 1882 and was hanged in November of that year. Richmond L. Clow, "A Dream Deferred: Crow Dog's Territorial Trials and the Push for Statehood," *South Dakota History* 37 (Spring 2007): 46, 66-69. *See also* Richmond L. Clow, "The Anatomy of a Lakota Shooting: Crow Dog and Spotted Tail, 1879-1881," *South Dakota History* 28 (Winter 1998): 209-27.

14. Andrews to Rosebud Agent, 14 July 1882, Fort Randall LS, no. 115.

15. Andrews to AAG, Department of Dakota, 25 June 1882, ibid., no. 95. This detailed report of the tornado is based on damage reports (the Indians' camp was "prostrated"), and on mentions of storms in the following sources: Reginald and Gladys Laubin, *The Indian Tipi: Its History, Construction, and Use* (Norman: University of Oklahoma Press, 1957), pp. 96-99, and Alice Fletcher, "Camping with the Sioux" (handwritten ms), MS 4558, Series 5, p. 111, Alice Fletcher and Frances La Flesche Papers, National Anthropological Archives, Smithsonian Institution, Washington, D.C. Fletcher's account of being inside a tipi during a storm is fictional, but I have no doubt that, as an ethnologist, her knowledge of Sioux life makes hers an accurate reconstruction.

16. Andrews to AAG, Department of Dakota, 25 June 1882, Fort Randall LS, no. 95.

17. Amelia Ives to Andrews, 1 July 1882, Fort Randall LR, no #.

18. Ives to Andrews, 8 May 1882 (received 13 May), ibid., no. 249.

19. Andrews to Ives, 15 May 1882, Fort Randall LS, no. 82; Ives to Andrews, 19 May 1882, Fort Randall LR, no. 267.

20. Ives to Andrews, 1 July 1882.

21. Ives to Andrews, 8 May 1882.

22. Hassett to Marty, 14 June 1882, BCIMR, roll 5, fr. 390.

23. Marty to Brouillet, 13 July 1882, BCIMR, roll 5, frs. 399-400.

24. Ibid., fr. 400, and 5 Aug. 1882, fr. 401; Francis Paul Prucha, *American Indian Policy in Crisis: Christian Reformers and the Indian, 1865-1900* (Norman: University of Oklahoma Press, 1976), pp. 46-47. For details of the Catholic church's perspective on the Peace Policy, *see* Mary Claudia Duratschek, *Crusading along Sioux Trails: A History of the Catholic Indian Missions of South Dakota* (Yankton, S.Dak.: Benedictine Convent of the Sacred Heart, 1947), pp. 14-32.

25. Enclosure (petition), Hassett to Brouillet, 15 Aug. 1882, BCIMR, roll 4, frs. 1244-47.

26. Marty to Brouillet, 5 Aug. 1882.

27. Joan Mark, *A Stranger in Her Native Land: Alice Fletcher and the American Indians* (Lincoln: University of Nebraska Press, 1988), p. 83.

28. Alice Fletcher, "The White Buffalo Festival of the Uncpapas," *Sixteenth and Seventeenth Annual Reports of the Trustees of the Peabody Museum of American Archaeology and Ethnology* 3 (1884): 260-75.

29. Ibid, p. 274n22.

30. Ibid., p. 275. *See also* Fletcher, "Camping with the Sioux," pp. 127-31, which contains a slightly different version of these events.

31. AAG, Department of Dakota, to Andrews, 12 Aug. 1882, Fort Randall LR, no. 419.

32. McLaughlin to Andrews, 21 Nov. 1881, ibid., no #; Andrews to McLaughlin, 29 July 1882, Fort Randall LS, no. 123.

CHAPTER 9. FORT RANDALL, AUGUST–OCTOBER 1882

1. Sitting Bull's drawings for Pratt and Tear can be found in Mathew Stirling, *Three Pictographic Autobiographies of Sitting Bull,* Smithsonian Miscellaneous Collections, vol. 97, no. 5 (Washington, D.C.: Smithso-

nian Institution, 1938), pp. 35-57. The Quimby drawings are found in Alexis A. Praus, *A New Pictographic Autobiography of Sitting Bull*, Smithsonian Miscellaneous Collections, vol. 123, no. 6 (Washington, D.C.: Smithsonian Institution, 1955).

2. Stirling, *Three Pictographic Autobiographies of Sitting Bull*, p. 37.

3. William John Armstrong, "Sitting Bull and a Michigan Family: Legacy of an Unlikely Friendship," *Michigan History Magazine* 79 (Jan.-Feb. 1995): 28-35.

4. Andrews to Rosebud and Pine Ridge agents, 7 Aug. 1882, Fort Randall LS, 2 Jan. 1882-19 July 1883, nos. 131, 132, Records of the United States Army Continental Commands, 1821-1920, RG 393, NARA, Washington, D.C.; Jerome A. Greene, *Fort Randall on the Missouri, 1856-1892* (Pierre: South Dakota State Historical Society Press, 2005), pp. 185-86.

5. Andrews to Pine Ridge agent, 7 Aug. 1882, no. 132; Andrews to CO, Fort Niobrara, 7 Aug. 1882, Fort Randall LS, no. 130.

6. Andrews to CO, Fort Hale, 7 Aug. 1882, ibid., no. 129; Andrews to CO, Fort Niobrara, 7 Aug. 1882.

7. Andrews to Rosebud agent, 7 Aug. 1882.

8. Greene, *Fort Randall on the Missouri*, p. 141.

9. Ibid., pp. 185-86.

10. For information on Grant's Peace Policy and the resultant education of the Indians, *see* Francis Paul Prucha, *American Indian Policy in Crisis: Christian Reformers and the Indian, 1865-1900* (Norman: University of Oklahoma Press, 1976). For more on Indian education to promote acculturation, *see* David Wallace Adams, *Education for Extinction: American Indians and the Boarding School Experience* (Lawrence: University Press of Kansas, 1995).

11. Joan Mark, *A Stranger in Her Native Land: Alice Fletcher and the American Indians* (Lincoln: University of Nebraska Press, 1988), p. 79. For more on Richard Pratt, *see* Donal F. Lindsey, *Indians at Hampton Institute, 1877-1923* (Urbana: University of Illinois Press, 1995), pp. 22-23, and Adams, *Education for Extinction*, pp. 36-51.

12. AAG, Department of Dakota, to Andrews, 9 Aug. 1882, Fort Randall LR, no. 404.

13. Telegram, Pratt to Andrews, 10 Aug. 1882, and Pratt to Andrews, 7 Aug. 1882, Fort Randall LR, nos. 405, 406; Andrews to Pratt, 12 Aug. 1882, Fort Randall LS, no. 140.

14. Andrews to Alice Fletcher, 17 Aug. 1882, Fort Randall LS, no. 142.

15. Andrews to AAG, Department of Dakota, 27 Aug. 1882, Fort Randall LS, no. 146.

16. Adams, *Education for Extinction*, pp. 121-35; George E. Hyde, *A Sioux Chronicle* (Norman: University of Oklahoma Press, 1956), pp. 53-57.

17. Andrews to AAG, Department of Dakota, 5 Sept. 1882, Fort Randall LS, no. 158.

18. Andrews to AAG, Department of Dakota, 27 Aug. 1882, ibid., no. 146.

19. CIA to SI, 22 Sept. 1882, Fort Randall LR, no. 523.

20. Endorsements, ibid., 28 Sept., 4, 6, 10 Oct. 1882.

21. Pratt to Andrews, 30 Oct. 1882, Fort Randall LR, no #; Luther Standing Bear, *My People the Sioux* (Boston: Houghton Mifflin Co., 1928), p. 161.

22. For more on Pratt's personality and his vision for the school, *see* Adams, *Education for Extinction*, pp. 51-55.

23. Standing Bear, *My People the Sioux*, p. 161.

24. Hare to Andrews, 28 Aug. 1882, Fort Randall LR, no #; Andrews to AAG, Department of Dakota, 5 Sept. 1882, Fort Randall LS, no. 158.

25. Andrews to Hare, 29 Aug. 1882, ibid., no. 148.

26. Andrews to AAG, Department of Dakota, 5 Sept. 1882.

27. Kinzie to Ridpath, 9 Apr. 1883, Fort Randall LS, no. 47. *See also* M. A. DeWolfe Howe, *The Life and Labors of Bishop Hare, Apostle to the Sioux* (New York: Sturgis & Walton Co., 1911), pp. 230-31.

28. Robinson to Andrews, 18 Sept. 1882, Fort Randall LR, no. 514; Hassett to Brouillet, 15 Aug. 1882, Bureau of Catholic Indian Missions Records, Marquette University Libraries, microfilm ed., roll 4, fr. 1244-47. For more on George Sword, *see* Mark R. Ellis, "Reservation *Akicitas*: The Pine Ridge Indian Police, 1879-1885," *South Dakota History* 29 (Fall 1999): 195-99, and Joshua Garrett-Davis, "Dakota Images: George Sword," ibid., p. 262.

29. Andrews to AAG, Department of Dakota, 5 Sept. 1882, Fort Randall LS, no. 158.

30. Lawson to AAG, Department of Dakota, 18 Oct. 1882, ibid., no. 182; AAG, Department of Dakota, to CO, Fort Randall, 21 Oct. 1882, Fort Randall LR, no. 538. Captain Gaines Lawson was the commanding officer at Fort Randall from 26 September to 8 November 1882. Greene, *Fort Randall on the Missouri*, p. 182.

31. George P. Ahern to Captain W. S. Campbell, 12 July 1929, Box 107,

Walter Stanley Campbell Collection, University of Oklahoma Libraries, Norman. Ahern may have learned to speak Lakota. In his letters, there is no mention of an interpreter present at his meetings with Sitting Bull, and the tone of his anecdotes gives the impression that he could speak to the chief directly.

32. Paul Richard to Sitting Bull, 12 Dec. 1883, Box 113, Campbell Collection. The letter, typed in French, was translated by Mary Hellen Rahal and refers to an earlier unanswered letter. It was found among Sitting Bull's effects after his death on 15 December 1890—a long time to keep a letter; perhaps Sitting Bull was waiting for the money to turn up.

33. Notation on Richard to Sitting Bull, 12 Dec. 1883; Stanley Vestal, *New Sources of Indian History, 1850-1891: A Miscellany* (Norman: University of Oklahoma Press, 1934), pp. 271-72; Ahern to Campbell, 12 July 1929.

34. Ahern to Campbell, 12, 31 July 1929, Box 107, Stanley Collection.

35. Ahern to Campbell, 12 July 1929.

36. Ibid. Ahern gives her age as ten, but both prisoner of war lists and the Standing Rock annual census indicate an age of five towards the end of 1882. *See* Ephriam Dickson, *Sitting Bull Surrender Census* (Pierre: South Dakota State Historical Society Press, 2010).

37. Ahern to Campbell, 12 July 1929.

38. Sitting Bull's family history is difficult, if not impossible, to ascertain, and variations in names complicates it further. My main source for the children's deaths is Robert M. Utley, *The Lance and the Shield: The Life and Times of Sitting Bull* (New York: Henry Holt & Co., 1993), pp. 22, 166, 193, 365n3. For the death of Sitting Bull's first son, *see* Interview of Henry Oscar One Bull, n.d., n.p., Box 104, Campbell Collection.

CHAPTER 10. FORT RANDALL, NOVEMBER 1882–JANUARY 1883

1. Post Returns, Sept. 1882, Records of the Adjutant General's Office, 1780s-1917, RG 94, NARA, Microfilm Publication M617, roll 990; Jerome A. Greene, *Fort Randall on the Missouri, 1856-1892* (Pierre: South Dakota State Historical Society Press, 2005), p. 182; AAG, Department of Dakota, to CO, Fort Randall, 2 Nov. 1882, and Endorsements, Swaine to AAG, Department of Dakota, 21 Nov. 1882, Fort Randall LR, no #s, Records of the United States Army Continental Commands, 1821-1920, RG 393, NARA, Washington, D.C.

2. Post Returns, Nov. 1882.

3. George P. Ahern to Capt. W. S. Campbell, 12 July 1929, Box 107, Walter Stanley Campbell Collection, Western History Collections, University of Oklahoma Libraries, Norman.

4. Ahern to Summerall, 20 June 1929, ibid.

5. Post Returns, Nov. 1882; William John Armstrong, "Sitting Bull and a Michigan Family: Legacy of an Unlikely Friendship," *Michigan History Magazine* 79 (Jan.-Feb. 1995): 32.

6. Special Post Return, 4 Dec. 1882; Swaine to AAG, Department of Dakota, 7 Dec. 1882, Fort Randall LS, no. 249, RG 393, NARA.

7. Swaine to AG, Department of Dakota, 2 Feb. 1883, Fort Randall LS, no. 20.

8. Ahern to Campbell, 31 July 1929, Box 107, Campbell Collection; Greene, *Fort Randall on the Missouri,* pp. 110-11; Robert M. Utley, *Frontier Regulars: The United States Army and the Indian* (New York: Macmillan Publishing Co., 1973), p. 26. The low rate of alcoholism in African American units was due in part to the discipline of their officers and to the religious nature of many of the soldiers.

9. Endorsement, Post trader to SW, 18 Nov. 1882, Fort Randall LS, no. 208.

10. Denny Moran, as told to Will G. Robinson, "Denny Moran's Reminiscences of Ft. Randall," *South Dakota Historical Collections* 23 (1947): 291-93.

11. Swaine to McLaughlin, 21 Nov. 1882, Fort Randall LS, no. 218; Frances Chamberlain Holley, *Once Their Home; or, Our Legacy from the Dahkotahs* (Chicago: Donohue & Henneberry, 1893), pp. 282-83.

12. One Bull's Memoirs, pp. 21-23, Box 104, Folder 11, Campbell Collection. *See also* Interview of Bob Tail Bull, n.p., n.d., Box 105, Folder 16.

13. Robert M. Utley, *The Lance and the Shield: The Life and Times of Sitting Bull* (New York: Henry Holt & Co., 1993), pp. 231, 263.

14. Ibid., pp. 23-24, 301.

15. Editorial, *Bismarck Tribune*, 10 Mar. 1882.

16. "An Urgent Request," ibid., 2 June 1882.

17. Quoted ibid.

18. Pettigrew, quoted in "The Sioux Reservation," ibid., 21 July 1882.

19. Louis L. Pfaller, *James McLaughlin: The Man with an Indian Heart* (New York: Vantage Press, 1978), p. 3; "Muloting Marauders," *Saint Paul and Minneapolis Pioneer Press*, 2 May 1883; A. L. Haydon, *The Riders of*

the Plains: Record of the Royal North-West Mounted Police of Canada, 1873-1910 (London: Andrew Melrose, 1910), p. 158.

20. The information on the Sioux Land Commission comes from George E. Hyde, *A Sioux Chronicle* (Norman: University of Oklahoma Press, 1956), pp. 107-44; George W. Kingsbury, *History of Dakota Territory*, and George M. Smith, *South Dakota: Its History and Its People*, 5 vols. (Chicago: S. J. Clarke Publishing Co., 1915): 2:1238-49; and U.S., Congress, Senate, *Report of the Select Committee to Examine into the Conditions of the Sioux and Crow Indians*, 48th Cong., 1st sess., 1884, S. Rep. 283, pp. xxxviii-xlv.

21. Pfaller, *James McLaughlin*, pp. 22-23, 48-53; James McLaughlin, *My Friend the Indian* (1910; reprint ed., Lincoln: University of Nebraska Press, 1989), pp. 40-52; Louis L. Pfaller, "The Brave Bear Murder Case," *North Dakota History* 36 (Spring 1969): 121-39. List B of the Indian prisoners of war (*see* note 20, Chapter 4 above) has the entry "Brave Bear's wife and child." *See also* Greene, *Fort Randall on the Missouri*, p. 189.

22. "Probable Suicide of Brave Bear," *Yankton Daily Press and Dakotaian*, 17 Nov. 1881.

23. Pfaller, "Brave Bear Murder Case," pp. 134-36; Robert H. Lowie, *Indians of the Plains* (Garden City, N.Y.: Natural History Press, 1954), pp. 117-18, 121-22; Pfaller, *James McLaughlin*, p. 53.

24. "United States Court," *Yankton Daily Press and Dakotaian*, 5 Jan. 1882.

25. Quoted in McLaughlin, *My Friend the Indian*, p. 40. There are a number of detailed references to the Brave Bear case in the *Yankton Daily Press and Dakotaian*, of which the following are the main ones: "Probable Suicide of Brave Bear," 17 Nov. 1881; "Guilty of Murder," 5 Jan. 1882; "Brave Bear Sentenced," 9 Jan. 1882; "The Ghastly Preparations," 14 Nov. 1882; and "Brave Bear Hung," 15 Nov. 1882. The last is a graphic account of the actual hanging.

26. J. B. Hassett to Martin Marty, 14 June 1882, Bureau of Catholic Indian Missions Records, Marquette University Libraries, microfilm ed., roll 5, fr. 390.

27. W. M. Ridpath to Swaine, 11 Dec. 1882, Fort Randall LR, no #.

28. Smith to Swaine, 16 Dec. 1882, ibid.

29. John S. Gray, "The Story of Mrs. Picotte-Galpin: A Sioux Heroine," *Montana, the Magazine of Western History* 36 (Summer 1986): 20.

30. Swaine to AAG, Department of Dakota, 8 Jan. 1883, Fort Randall LS, no. 6; Endorsement, Terry to CO, Fort Randall, 12 Jan. 1883, Fort Randall LR, no. 288.

31. Swaine to AG, Department of Dakota, 30 Jan. 1883, Fort Randall LS, no. 19; Second Endorsement, McLaughlin to Terry, 30 Mar. 1883, and Third Endorsement, AAG, Department of Dakota, to Swaine, 4 Apr. 1883, both Fort Randall LR, no. 826. The woman who remarried was the wife of Charging Bear, who said that her ex-husband had another wife with him when he left Fort Yates.

CHAPTER 11. RELEASE FROM FORT RANDALL

1. Rudolf Cronau to CIA, 27 Jan. 1882, doc. no. 1826, James McLaughlin Papers, Assumption College Archives, Richardton, N.Dak. (hereafter McLaughlin Papers), microfilm ed., roll 32.

2. Strike-the-Ree to SW, Yankton Agency, 11 Dec. 1882, doc. no. 23099, ibid.

3. Lincoln to SI, 20 Dec. 1882, doc. no. 23099, ibid.

4. For examples of Williamson's efforts on behalf of Sitting Bull, *see* William to Andrews, 12 Dec. 1881, Fort Randall LR, no #, Records of the United States Army Continental Commands, 1821-1920, RG 393, NARA, Washington, D.C.; Winifred W. Barton, *John P. Williamson: A Brother to the Sioux* (New York: Fleming H. Revell Co., 1919), pp. 167-68.

5. *See*, for example, Williamson to Andrews, 12 Dec. 1881, Fort Randall LR, no #; Martin Marty to Brouillet, 13 July 1882, Bureau of Catholic Indian Missions Records, Marquette University Libraries, microfilm ed., roll 5, fr. 399; Andrews to AAG, Department of Dakota, 4, 25 July 1882, Fort Randall LS, nos. 104, 158, RG 393, NARA.

6. McLaughlin to Price, 15 Feb. 1883, copy in Fort Randall LR, no. 32; James McLaughlin, *My Friend the Indian* (1910; reprint ed., Lincoln: University of Nebraska Press, 1989), pp. 134-35.

7. McLaughlin to Price, 15 Feb. 1883.

8. Price to SI, 21 Feb. 1883, copy in Fort Randall LR, no. 32.

9. Teller to SW, 23 Feb. 1883, copy ibid.

10. Lincoln to SI, 15 Mar. 1883, SW, LS, Records of the Office of the Secretary of War, RG 107, NARA, Microfilm Publication M6, roll 87, fr. 164.

11. Drum to Commanding General, Military Division of the Missouri, 17 Mar. 1883, copy in Fort Randall LR, no. 32.

12. Willliams to Terry, 20 Mar. 1883, ibid.

13. "Sitting Bull to be Removed," *Yankton Daily Press and Dakotaian*, 21 Mar. 1883.

14. James McLaughlin to "My dear Captain," 25 Apr. 1883, McLaughlin Papers, roll 20, fr. 131; Robert M. Utley, *The Lance and the Shield: The Life and Times of Sitting Bull* (New York: Henry Holt & Co., 1993), p. 3.

15. Swaine to McLaughlin, Fort Randall, 13 Apr. 1883, McLaughlin Papers, roll 2, frs. 208-9. For some unknown reason, crosses were put against the names of Bone Tomahawk, The-Man-That-Takes-The-Gun-Away, and Fur Coat.

16. Kinzie to McLaughlin, 9 Apr. 1883, Fort Randall LS, no. 48.

17. Kinzie to Ridpath, 9 Apr. 1883, Fort Randall LS, no. 47.

18. Quoted in M. A. DeWolfe Howe, *The Life and Labors of Bishop Hare, Apostle to the Sioux* (New York: Sturgis & Walton Co., 1911), pp. 230-31.

19. Utley, *Lance and the Shield*, p. 246; Post Returns, Fort Randall, Sept. 1881-May 1883, Records of the Adjutant General's Office, 1780s-1917, RG 94, NARA, Microfilm Publication M617, roll 990. For more on Grant Marsh, *see* Joseph Mills Hanson, *The Conquest of the Missouri: Being the Story of the Life and Exploits of Captain Grant Marsh* (Chicago: A. C. McClurg & Co., 1909). For Marsh's trip with the wounded from the Little Bighorn, *see* pp. 301-6.

20. Post Returns, Fort Randall, April 1883.

21. Hanson, *Conquest of the Missouri*, p. 415.

22. "Sitting Bull Interviewed," *Chamberlain Register,* reprinted in *Yankton Daily Press and Dakotaian*, 8 May 1883.

23. "Dakota," *Saint Paul and Minneapolis Daily Pioneer Press*, 10 May 1883; Frank H. Goodyear III, "Wanted: Sitting Bull and His Photographic Portrait," *South Dakota History* 40 (Summer 2010): 144-45. This photograph is sometimes assigned a later date.

24. Hanson, *Conquest of the Missouri*, pp. 416-17.

25. "Sitting Bull at Home," *Yankton Daily Press and Dakotaian*, May 14, 1883.

26. Post Returns, Fort Randall, Apr. 1883; "Sitting Bull at Home," *Yankton Daily Press and Dakotaian*, 14 May 1883. Sources give different numbers for the Hunkpapas arriving at Standing Rock. The post return is the most reliable. Taking into account the four deaths and one birth that took place during the journey, I calculate that 149 people arrived at Standing Rock.

27. Sitting Bull, quoted in "Sitting Bull at Home."

28. McLaughlin, quoted in "Revised Standing Rock," *Saint Paul and Minneapolis Daily Pioneer Press*, 26 May 1883.

29. "Revised Standing Rock." For McLaughlin's report, *see* Louis L. Pfaller, *James McLaughlin: The Man with an Indian Heart* (New York: Vantage Press, 1978), pp. 96, 98.

30. "Revised Standing Rock."

31. Pfaller, *James McLaughlin*, p. 96.

32. "Revised Standing Rock."

33. Ibid.; Pfaller, *James McLaughlin*, p. 98.

34. Quoted in Pfaller, *James McLaughlin*, p. 98.

35. "Revised Standing Rock."

36. Utley, *Lance and the Shield*, p. 254.

37. Report to the Secretary of the Interior, Standing Rock Agency, 20 Nov. 1889, McLaughlin Papers, doc. no. 34694, roll 33; Utley, *Lance and the Shield*, p. 255; Pfaller, *James McLaughlin*, pp. 89-94.

EPILOGUE

1. Quoted in *Sitting Bull and the Paradox of Lakota Nationhood*, by Gary C. Anderson (New York: Harper Collins College Publishers, 1996), p. 138.

2. Louis L. Pfaller, *James McLaughlin: The Man with an Indian Heart* (New York: Vantage Press, 1978), pp. 99-107; Robert M. Utley, *The Lance and the Shield: The Life and Times of Sitting Bull* (New York: Henry Holt & Co., 1993), p. 266.

3. Utley, *Lance and the Shield*, pp. 257-58.

4. Ibid., pp. 272-80; Herbert T. Hoover, "The Sioux Agreement of 1889 and Its Aftermath," *South Dakota History* 19 (Spring 1989): 58.

5. Pfaller, *James McLaughlin*, pp. 127-65; Utley, *Lance and the Shield*, pp. 291-307, 313.

BIBLIOGRAPHY

MANUSCRIPT MATERIALS AND COLLECTIONS

Bureau of Catholic Indian Missions. Records. Microfilm ed. Marquette University, Milwaukee, Wis.

Campbell, Walter Stanley, Collection. Western History Collections, University of Oklahoma Libraries, Norman, Okla.

Fletcher, Alice C., and Frances La Flesche Papers. National Anthropological Archives, Smithsonian Institution, Washington, D.C.

Fletcher, Alice Cunningham. "Camping with the Sioux: Fieldwork Diary." National Anthropological Archives, Smithsonian Institution, www.nmnh.si.edu/naa/fletcher.

McLaughlin, James, Papers. Microfilm ed. Assumption College Archives, Richardton, N.Dak.

National Archives, Washington, D.C.

Record Group 48. Records of the Office of the Secretary of the Interior, 1849-1903. Microfilm Publication M606 (Letters Sent), rolls 26-27.

Record Group 75. Records of the Bureau of Indian Affairs. Microfilm Publication M595 (Indian Census Rolls, 1885-1940), roll 547.

Record Group 94. Records of the Adjutant General's Office, 1780s-1917. Microfilm Publication M617 (Post Returns), roll 990.

Record Group 107. Records of the Office of the Secretary of War. Microfilm Publication M6 (Letters Sent), rolls 82-84, 87.

Record Group 393. Records of the United States Army Continental Commands, 1821-1920, Microfilm Publication M1495 (Special Files, Division of the Missouri), rolls 3-5.

BOOKS AND ARTICLES

Athearn, Robert G. *Forts of the Upper Missouri*. Englewood Cliffs, N.J.: Prentice-Hall, 1967.

Anderson, Gary C. *Little Crow: Spokesman for the Sioux*. Saint Paul: Minnesota Historical Society Press, 1986.

——. *Sitting Bull and the Paradox of Lakota Nationhood*. New York: Harper Collins College Publishers, 1996.

169

Armstrong, William John. "Sitting Bull and a Michigan Family: Legacy of an Unlikely Friendship." *Michigan History* 79 (Jan.-Feb. 1995): 28-35.

Adams, David Wallace. *Education for Extinction: American Indians and the Boarding School Experience, 1875-1928*. Lawrence: University of Kansas, 1995.

Bailey, Dix, and Mead (copyright holders). "Sitting Bull Collection," *South Dakota History* 5 (Summer 1975): 245-65.

Barrett, Carole. "One Bull: A Man of Good Understanding" *North Dakota History* 66 (Summer/Fall 1999): 3-16.

Barton, Winifred W. *John P. Williamson: A Brother to the Sioux*. New York: Fleming H. Revell Co., 1919.

Berg, Francie M. *The Last Great Buffalo Hunts*. Hettinger, N.Dak.: Dakota Buttes Visitors Council, 1995.

Boyes, W. *Custer's Black White Man*. Washington, D.C.: Walbenjon Associates, 1972.

Boyton, Paul. *The Story of Paul Boyton: A Rare Tale of Travel and Adventure*. London: George Routledge & Sons, 1893.

Bray, Kingsley M. "Before Sitting Bull: Interpreting Hunkpapa Political History, 1750-1867." *South Dakota History* 40 (Summer 2010): 97-135.

———. *Crazy Horse: A Lakota Life*. Civilization of the American Indian Series, vol. 254. Norman: University of Oklahoma Press, 2006.

Brouillet, J. B. A. "Abbot Martin Visits Sitting Bull." *Annals of the Catholic Indian Missions* 2 (Jan. 1878): 7-10.

Burdick, Usher L. *Tales from Buffalo Land: The Story of Fort Buford*. Baltimore: Wirth Bros., 1940.

Calvert, Patricia. *Standoff at Standing Rock: The Story of Sitting Bull and James McLaughlin*. Brookfield, Conn.: Twenty-First Century Books, 2001.

Carley, Kenneth. *The Dakota War of 1862: Minnesota's Other Civil War*. Saint Paul: Minnesota Historical Society Press, 1976.

Carlson, Paul N. *The Plains Indians*. Elma Dill Russell Spencer Series in the West and Southwest, no. 19. College Station: Texas A & M University Press, 1998.

Clark, W. P. *The Indian Sign Language, with Brief Explanatory Notes, . . . Signals of Our Aborigines*. Philadelphia: L. R. Hamersly & Co., 1885.

Clow, Richmond L. "The Anatomy of a Lakota Shooting: Crow Dog and

Spotted Tail, 1879-1881." *South Dakota History* 28 (Winter 1998): 209-27.

——. "A Dream Deferred: Crow Dog's Territorial Trials and the Push for Statehood." *South Dakota History* 37 (Spring 2007): 46-73.

Cozzens, Peter, ed. *Eyewitnesses to the Indian Wars, 1865-1890: The Long War for the Northern Plains*. Mechanicsburg, Pa.: Stackpole Books, 2004.

Cronau, Rudolf. "My Visit among the Hostile Dakota Indians and How They Became My Friends." *South Dakota Historical Collections* 22 (1946): 410-25.

Creelman, James. *On the Great Highway: The Wanderings and Adventures of a Special Correspondent*. Boston: Lothrop Publishing Co., 1901.

DeLand, Charles Edmund. "The Sioux Wars," *South Dakota Historical Collections* 17 (1934): 177-551.

DeMallie, Raymond J. "The Sioux in Dakota and Montana Territories: Cultural and Historical Background of the Ogden B. Read Collection." In *Vestiges of a Proud Nation: The Ogden B. Read Northern Plains Indian Collection*. Ed. Glenn E. Markoe. Pp. 19-69. Burlington, Vt.: Robert Hull Fleming Museum, 1986.

Densmore, Frances. *Teton Sioux Music*. 1918. Reprint ed. New York: Da Capo Press, 1972.

Dick, Everett. *The Sod House Frontier*. New York: D. Appleton-Century Co., 1937.

Dickson, Ephriam D., III. *Sitting Bull Surrender Census*. Pierre: South Dakota State Historical Society Press, 2010.

Diessner, Don. *There Are No Indians Left But Me!: Sitting Bull's Story*. El Segundo, Calif.: Upton & Sons, 1993.

Dorsey, James Owen. "Siouan Sociology." In *Fifteenth Annual Report of the Bureau of Ethnology to the Secretary of the Smithsonian Institution, 1893-'94*. Washington, D.C.: Government Printing Office, 1897.

Duratschek, Mary Claudia. *Crusading along Sioux Trails: A History of the Catholic Indian Missions of South Dakota*. Yankton, S.Dak.: Benedictine Convent of the Sacred Heart, 1947.

Ellis, Mark R. "Reservation *Akicitas*: The Pine Ridge Indian Police, 1879-1885." *South Dakota History* 29 (Fall 1999): 185-210.

Fletcher, Alice C. "Sun Dance of the Ogallala Sioux." *Proceedings of the American Association for the Advancement of Science* 30 (1883): 580-84.

———. "The White Buffalo Festival of the Uncpapas." *Sixteenth and Seventeenth Annual Reports of the Trustees of the Peabody Museum of American Archaeology and Ethnology* 3 (1884): 260-75.

Garrett-Davis, Joshua. "Dakota Images: George Sword." *South Dakota History* 29 (Fall 1999): 262.

Goodyear, Frank. "The Narratives of Sitting Bull's Surrender: Bailey, Dix, and Mead's Photographic Western." In *Dressing in Feathers: The Construction of the Indian in American Popular Culture.* Ed. S. Elizabeth Bird. Pp. 29-43. Boulder, Colo.: Westview Press, 1996.

Goodyear, Frank H., III. "Wanted: Sitting Bull and His Photographic Portrait." *South Dakota History* 40 (Summer 2010): 136-62.

Gray, John S. "The Story of Mrs. Picotte-Galpin." *Montana, the Magazine of Western History* 36 (Spring 1986): 2-21; (Summer 1986): 2-21.

Greene, Jerome A. *Fort Randall on the Missouri, 1856-1892.* Pierre: South Dakota State Historical Society Press, 2005.

Haydon, A. L. *The Riders of the Plains: Record of the Royal North-West Mounted Police of Canada, 1873-1910.* London: Andrew Melrose, 1910.

Hanson, Joseph Mills. *The Conquest of the Missouri: Being the Story of the Life and Exploits of Captain Grant Marsh.* Chicago: A. C. McClurg & Co., 1909.

Hassrick, Royal B. *The Sioux: Life and Customs of a Warrior Society.* Norman: University of Oklahoma Press, 1963.

Heitman, Francis B. *Historical Register and Dictionary of the United States Army, from Its Organization, September 29, 1789, to March 2, 1903.* 2 vols. Washington D.C.: Government Printing Office, 1903.

Hedren, Paul L. "Sitting Bull's Surrender at Fort Buford: An Episode in American History." *North Dakota History* 62 (Fall 1995): 2-15.

Hoig, Stan. *Perilous Pursuit: The U.S. Cavalry and the Northern Cheyennes.* Boulder: University Press of Colorado, 2002.

Holley, Frances Chamberlain. *Once Their Home; or, Our Legacy from the Dahkotahs.* Chicago: Donohue & Henneberry, 1893.

Hoover, Herbert T. "The Sioux Agreement of 1889 and Its Aftermath." *South Dakota History* 19 (Spring 1989): 56-94.

Howard, James H. "Dakota Winter Counts as a Source of Plains History." In *Anthropological Papers, Numbers 57-62,* Smithsonian Institution,

Bureau of American Ethnology, Bulletin no. 173. Washington, D.C.: Government Printing Office, 1960.

Howe, M. A. DeWolfe. *The Life and Labors of Bishop Hare: Apostle to the Sioux*. New York: Sturgis & Walton Co., 1914.

Hurt, Wesley R, and William E. Lass. *Frontier Photographer: Stanley Morrow's Dakota Years*. University of South Dakota and University of Nebraska Press, 1936.

Hyde, George E. *Red Cloud's Folk: A History of the Oglala Sioux Indians*. Norman: University of Oklahoma Press, 1975.

——. *A Sioux Chronicle*. Norman: University of Oklahoma Press, 1956.

Jackson, Brenda K. "Holding Down the Fort: A History of Dakota Territory's Fort Randall." *South Dakota History* 32 (Spring 2002): 1-27.

Kappler, Charles J., comp. *Indian Affairs: Laws and Treaties*, Vol. II: *Treaties*. Washington, D.C.: Government Printing Office, 1904.

Karolevitz, Robert F. *Bishop Martin Marty: "The Black Robe Lean Chief."* Yankton, S.Dak.: By the Author, 1980.

Kingsbury, George W., and George M. Smith. *History of Dakota Territory* and *South Dakota: Its History and Its People*, 5 vols. Chicago: S. J. Clarke Publishing Co., 1915.

Laubin, Reginald and Gladys. *The Indian Tipi: Its History, Construction, and Use*. Norman: University of Oklahoma Press, 1957.

Laviolette, Gontran. *The Sioux Indians in Canada* Regina: Marian Press, 1944.

Lindsey, Donal F. *Indians at Hampton Institute, 1877-1923*. Urbana: University of Illinois Press, 1995.

Lowie, Robert H. *Indians of the Plains*. Garden City, N.Y.: Natural History Press, 1963.

MacEwan, Grant. *Sitting Bull: The Years in Canada*. Edmonton, Alberta: Hurtig Publishers, 1973.

McLaughlin, James. *My Friend the Indian*. 1910. Reprint ed. Lincoln: University of Nebraska Press, 1989.

Manzione, Joseph, *"I Am Looking to the North for My Life": Sitting Bull 1876-1881*. Salt Lake City: University of Utah Press, 1991.

Mark, Joan. *A Stranger in Her Native Land: Alice Fletcher and the American Indians*. Lincoln: University of Nebraska Press, 1988.

Mathes, Valerie Sherer, and Richard Lowitt. *The Standing Bear Controversy: Prelude to Indian Reform*. Urbana: University of Illinois Press, 2003.

Moran, Denny, as told to Will G. Robinson. "Denny Moran's Reminiscences of Ft. Randall," *South Dakota Historical Collections* 23 (1947): 266-306.

Nankivell, John H. *Buffalo Soldier Regiment: History of the Twenty-fifth United States Infantry, 1869-1926.* Bison Books ed. Lincoln: University of Nebraska Press, 2001.

Nurge, Ethel, ed. *The Modern Sioux: Social Systems and Reservation Culture.* Lincoln: University of Nebraska Press, 1970.

Pfaller, Louis L. "The Brave Bear Murder Case." *North Dakota History* 36 (Spring 1969): 121-39.

——. "The Galpin Journal: Dramatic Record of an Odyssey of Peace." *Montana, the Magazine of Western History* 18 (Apr. 1968): 2-23.

——. *James McLaughlin: The Man with an Indian Heart.* New York: Vantage Press, 1978.

Praus, Alexis A. *A New Pictographic Autobiography of Sitting Bull.* Smithsonian Miscellaneous Collections, vol. 123, no. 6. Washington, D.C.: Smithsonian Institution, 1955.

Prucha, Francis Paul. *American Indian Policy in Crisis: Christian Reformers and the Indian, 1865-1900.* Norman, University of Oklahoma Press, 1976.

——. *American Indian Treaties: The History of a Political Anomaly.* Berkeley: University of California Press, 1994.

Remele, Larry, ed. *Fort Buford and the Military Frontier of the Northern Plains, 1850-1900.* Bismarck: State Historical Society of North Dakota, 1987.

Rickey, Don, Jr. *Forty Miles a Day on Beans and Hay: The Enlisted Soldier Fighting the Indian Wars.* Norman: University of Oklahoma Press, 1963.

Riggs, Stephen R. *Dakota Grammar, Texts, and Ethnography.* Smithsonian Institution, Bureau of American Ethnology, Contributions to North American Ethnology, vol. 9. Washington, D.C.: Government Printing Office, 1893.

Robertson, R. G. *Rotting Face: Smallpox and the American Indian.* Caldwell, Idaho: Caxton Press, 2001.

Sajna, Mike. *Crazy Horse: The Life behind the Legend.* New York: John Wiley & Sons, 2000.

Smith, Decost. *Red Indian Experiences.* London: George Allen & Unwin, 1949.

Standing Bear, Luther. *Land of the Spotted Eagle*. Boston: Houghton Mifflin Co., 1933.

——. *My People the Sioux*. Boston: Houghton Mifflin Co., 1928.

Stirling, Mathew. *Three Pictographic Autobiographies of Sitting Bull*. Smithsonian Miscellaneous Collections, vol. 97, no. 5. Washington, D.C.: Smithsonian Institution, 1938.

Taylor, Joseph Henry. *Frontier and Indian Life and Kaleidoscopic Lives*. Valley City, N.Dak.: Washburn's Fiftieth Anniversary Committee, 1932.

Tibbles, Thomas Henry. *Buckskin and Blanket Days*: *Memoirs of a Friend of the Indians*. New York: Doubleday & Co., 1957.

U.S. Congress. Senate. *Report of the Select Committee to Examine into the Conditions of the Sioux and Crow Indians*. 48th Cong., 1st sess. 1884. S. Rep. 283.

Utley, Robert M. *Frontier Regulars: The United States Army and the Indian, 1866-1891*. New York: Macmillan Publishing Co., 1973.

——. *The Lance and the Shield: The Life and Times of Sitting Bull*. New York: Henry Holt & Co., 1993.

VanEpps-Taylor, Betti. *Forgotten Lives: African Americans in South Dakota*. Pierre: South Dakota State Historical Society Press, 2008.

Vestal, Stanley. *New Sources of Indian History, 1850-1891: A Miscellany*. Norman: University of Oklahoma Press, 1934.

——. *Sitting Bull, Champion of the Sioux: A Biography*. 1932. Reprint ed. Norman: University of Oklahoma Press, 1957.

Wade, F. C. "The Surrender of Sitting Bull: Jean Louis Legare's Story." *Canadian Magazine of Politics, Science, Art and Literature* 24 (Nov. 1904-Apr. 1905): 335-44.

Wagner, Sally Roesch, ed. *Daughters of Dakota, Volume II: Stories from the Attic*. Yankton, S.Dak.: By the Editor, 1990.

——, ed. *Daughters of Dakota, Vol. III: Stories of Friendship between the Settlers and the Dakota Indians*. Yankton, S.Dak.: By the Editor, 1990.

Walker, James R. *Lakota Belief and Ritual*. Ed. Raymond J. DeMallie and Elaine A. Jahner. Lincoln: University of Nebraska Press, 1980.

——. *Lakota Society*. Ed. Raymond J. DeMallie. Lincoln: University of Nebraska Press, 1982.

——."The Sun Dance and Other Ceremonies of the Ogalala Division of the Teton Dakota." *American Museum of Natural History Anthropological Papers* 16 (1917): 60-120.

NEWSPAPERS

Bismarck Tribune, 1880-1885.

Saint Paul and Minneapolis Pioneer Press, 1881-1883.

Yankton Daily Press & Dakotan, 1881-1884.

INDEX

Photograph inserts are unnumbered pages. A list of the illustrations can be found on page viii.

Great Sioux Reservation: buffalo hunts on, 34-35, 89-90; council of chiefs, 109; creation of, 3; Indian agencies, 23; sale of "surplus" lands, 115-18, 136-37
Greene, Jerome A., ix
Grey Eagle, 114-15
Gros Ventre Indians, 100

Hairy Coat (Man-who-Wears-Fur-Coat), 78-79, 121, 127
Half-a-Breechcloth band, 143n3
Hampton Normal and Agricultural Institute, 79-80, 102
Hare, William H. ("Swift Bird," *Zitkana duzahan*), 69-70, 77-80, 128
Harmon, Lulu Picotte, 20
Harmon, William, 20
Harrison, Benjamin, 137
Hassett, J. B., 93-94
Health and medical care: by army doctors, 44, 45, 143n4; of Gertie Bell, 92-93, 106; of Sitting Bull, 136; death and childbirth, 88; smallpox vaccinations, 83-84
Henderson, E. A., Mrs., 25
Her-Holy-Door, 41
Her-Lodge-in-Sight, 41, 44
Hidatsa Indians, 1, 83
High-as-the-Clouds, 18
High Bull, 121
Hinman, Samuel D., 117
Hin-zi-win. See Gertie Bell
His-Holy-Pipe, 127
Horse-raids, 1, 28, 72
Howe, Henry S., 40

Hump, 36
Hunkpapa (Uncapapa) Lakota Indians: band organization of, 143n3; as part of Sioux confederacy, 1-2; photographic documentation of, 85-86; reuniting of Sitting Bull's band, 56-57, 70, 121; at Standing Rock Agency, 14, 23. *See also* Bad Bows (*Itazipe Sica* band)
Hunting-His-Lodge, 27

Ilges, Guido, 10, 11
Indian boarding schools. *See* Education of children; Carlisle Indian Industrial School; Hampton Normal and Agricultural Institute
Indian Territory, 36, 62
Inkpaduta, 2
Iron Heart, 127
Ista-masa. See Cronau, Rudolf
Ives, Amelia, 78, 92-93

Johnson, Joseph, 118-19, 159n13
Jumping Bull, 27
Jumping Bull (Little Assiniboine), 10, 71-72, 114-15

Kelley, R. L., 130
Killed (grandson of White Dog), 102
Kimball, James, 147n8
Kinzie, George, 127
Kirkwood, Samuel J., 37

Lakota (Western Sioux) Indians: army expeditions against, 2-4; 181

10971253R00097